Mormons Answered
Verse by Verse

Mormons

Answered Verse by Verse

DAVID A. REED
and
JOHN R. FARKAS

But this man [Jesus Christ], because he continueth ever, hath an unchangeable priesthood. Wherefore he is able to save them to the uttermost that come unto God by him, seeing he ever liveth to make intercession for them.
——*Hebrews 7:24-25*

BAKER BOOK HOUSE
Grand Rapids, Michigan 49516

Copyright 1992 by
Baker Book House Company

ISBN: 0-8010-7761-3

Second printing, February 1993

Printed in the United States of America

To
Wesley Preston Walters
1926–1990

On November 9, 1990, the Reverend Wesley P. Walters was called home to be with the Lord.

He was pastor of the Marissa Presbyterian Church in Marissa, Illinois, since 1957.

Rev. Walters is best known in the counter-cult mission field for his research into the early history of the Mormon Church and for discovering the "Joseph Smith the Glass Looker" Bainbridge, New York, trial documents. He spent much of his free time searching in musty basements for documents concerning Joseph Smith and the beginnings of Mormonism.

His knowledge of Mormonism and the Bible were astounding. He truly was a living computer and shared his vast knowledge freely for the love of Christ.

Wesley P. Walters will be sorely missed.

Contents

Acknowledgments   9
Introduction   11

1. A Capsule History of Mormonism   15
2. What the Mormon Church Teaches   21
3. Mormon Scripture   27
4. Verse-by-Verse Answers for Mormons:
   Old Testament   37
      Genesis   37
      Exodus   45
      Deuteronomy   48
      Nehemiah   51
      Psalms   52
      Isaiah   55
      Jeremiah   57
      Ezekiel   58
      Daniel   59
      Amos   63
5. Verse-by-Verse Answers for Mormons:
   New Testament   65
      Matthew   65
      Luke   68
      John   71
      Acts   76
      Romans   82
      1 Corinthians   83
      2 Corinthians   88

Galatians   89
Ephesians   91
2 Thessalonians   94
1 Timothy   95
Hebrews   96
James   99
1 John   101
Revelation   102

6. Verse-by-Verse Answers for Mormons: Book of
   Mormon   105
      1 Nephi   106
      2 Nephi   111
      Jacob   112
      Mosiah   115
      Alma   115
      3 Nephi   116
      Mormon   118
      Ether   119
      Moroni   120

7. Some Techniques for Sharing the Gospel with
   Mormons   121

8. Testimonies of the Authors   129
   Notes   139
   Recommended Reading   143
   Subject Index   147
   Scripture Index   151
   Mormon Scripture Index   155

Acknowledgments

We would like to thank Phyllis Farkas for her insightful comments and corrections to the manuscript, and Penni Reed for her patient endurance.

Also, we have special thanks and gratitude to the writers and researchers who went before us for making their information available for our use.

But above all we thank our Lord and Savior Jesus Christ for giving us this opportunity to witness for the truth of his gospel.

Introduction

For some years the Mormon Church, officially the Church of Jesus Christ of Latter-day Saints, has been working hard for acceptance as a "mainline" Christian denomination. To a large extent that is how the general public now views it. We are accustomed to their TV ads portraying closely-knit families who worship together and uphold traditional values, and many Christians can be found playing favorite pieces of Christmas music sung by the Mormon Tabernacle Choir.

Yet, few realize how great a turnaround this represents. About a century ago Mormonism was locked in a life-or-death struggle with the American public over the issues of polygamy and the church's temporal power. In 1844 founder Joseph Smith died in a blazing gun battle, amid circumstances that threatened to pit the armed Mormon militia of Nauvoo (Illinois' second-largest city) against forces from surrounding towns and neighboring states. To avoid open conflict, in 1846 Brigham Young led a migration westward, only to have warfare threaten again by the mid-1850s. At that time the United States Army was actually advancing on Utah to use force, if necessary, to replace Brigham Young as territorial governor. The Utah militia never did engage the army, but more than 120 non-Mormons were killed by Mormons and their Indian allies in the infamous Mountain Meadows Massacre in 1857. In 1889 Mormon leaders were fugitives from justice, operating underground after the United States Congress declared them outlaws, dissolved the LDS Church corporation, and seized its property through the antipolygamy Edmunds-Tucker Act of 1887.

In 1890 Congress was drafting legislation to disenfranchise all Mormons in the United States, but relented when Church President Wilford Woodruff issued a Manifesto instructing believers to obey the law of the land rather than continue the practice of polygamy. That move ended much of the anti-Mormon hostility and opened the way for Utah's admission to the Union. It also began a long and largely successful campaign to rehabilitate the church's public image.

But, has the Mormon Church itself really changed that much, or have the changes been chiefly cosmetic for public consumption? Although it presents a mask of monotheism, LDS theology is still polytheistic.[1] Although Mormon men are required to obey the law and limit themselves to one wife, the scripture they use still shows God's favor on plural marriage.[2] Although Jesus Christ is given prominence in Mormon worship, this is not the same Jesus Christ known to Bible-reading Christians. In fact, many other familiar-sounding names and words take on different meanings for those fully initiated in LDS beliefs.

The sacred and secret rites performed in Mormon temples are strictly off limits to outsiders, or *gentiles* in the insiders' terminology, and are even off limits to members who have not qualified for a "temple recommend" from their local leadership. And, just as few outsiders are aware of the temple garments that temple Mormons wear constantly underneath ordinary street clothes, so also few are aware that Mormonism is actually a "wolf in sheep's clothing" (Matt. 7:15).

From around 200 thousand members in 1890 the Latter-day Saints have grown to over 8 million strong today, worldwide. Brigham Young University projects that there will be more than 265 million Mormons by A.D. 2080, if the present growth rate continues. With polygamous marriage discontinued more than a century ago, it becomes obvious that conversions account for a sizable amount of the increase, both past and projected. LDS television advertisements are effective, and so are the visits by pairs of young missionaries who arrive by bicycle, scriptures in hand, at doors across the United States.

No, it is not the Book of Mormon that these missionaries open to persuade potential converts, at least not at first; rather, it is the

Bible that furnishes dozens of citations the missionaries use to "prove" all other churches false and to reveal their own organization as the restoration of Christ's true church today. It is to refute this misuse of the Bible that *Mormons Answered Verse by Verse* is written.

1

A Capsule History of Mormonism

1805   Joseph Smith, Jr., is born on December 23rd in Sharon, Vermont, the fourth child of Lucy Mack and Joseph Smith.

1820   Joseph Smith, Jr., allegedly receives his First Vision in which God the Father and Jesus appear and tell him that the churches are all wrong and corrupt, their creeds an abomination in God's sight.

1823   The angel Moroni (or Nephi according to some accounts) allegedly appears to Smith and tells him of a history recorded on golden plates.

1826   New York legal records in *The People vs. Joseph Smith The Glass Looker*, dated March 20, 1826, reveal that he was brought to trial on charges of money digging—using a "peep stone" to locate hidden treasure.

1827   Guided by the angel Moroni, Smith allegedly unearths the golden plates of the Book of Mormon on Hill Cumorah in Manchester, New York.

1829   John the Baptist allegedly appears in Pennsylvania on May 15 and confers the Aaronic Priesthood on Joseph Smith, Jr., and his scribe Oliver Cowdery.

1829/   The Melchizedek Priesthood is allegedly given to Joseph
1830   Smith and Oliver Cowdery by the apostles Peter, James, and John.

1830   The Book of Mormon is published in Palmyra, New York.

1830   On April 6, Smith, with his brothers Hyrum and Samuel and friends Oliver Cowdery and David and Peter Whitmer, Jr., establish "The Church of Christ."

1831   The new church moves to Kirtland, Ohio, near Cleveland, where it grows to almost 1600 affiliates.

1833   Smith and company are violently expelled from Jackson County, Missouri.

1833   Smith's first sixty-five revelations are published as the *Book of Commandments*.

1834   The name of the church is changed to The Church of the Latter Day Saints.

1835   Practice of polygamy is publicly denied.

1835   Doctrine and Covenants is published as a major revision of the *Book of Commandments*.

1836   The first Mormon temple is built in Kirtland, Ohio.

1837   Mormon exodus from Kirtland, Ohio.

1838   The name of the church is changed to The Church of Jesus Christ of Latter-day Saints.

1838   About nineteen Mormon men, women, and children are killed by non-Mormons at Hauns Mill, Missouri.

1839   Mormons are driven from Missouri and take refuge in Illinois.

1840   LDS Church claims 30,000 members.

1840   Mormons found the city of Nauvoo, Illinois.

1842   Joseph Smith publicly denies charges of polygamy while secretly practicing it.

1843   Smith allegedly receives a divine revelation, recorded on July 12, approving polygamy (but the revelation is not added to Doctrine and Covenants until 1876, over thirty years later).

1844   Nauvoo becomes the second largest city in Illinois, after Chicago. Joseph Smith is mayor and lieutenant-general of the militia.

1844   *The Nauvoo Expositor* publishes its first and only issue on June 7—an exposé of Mormon polygamy in Nauvoo, Illinois.

1844   On June 10, acting on the orders of the Nauvoo City Council and Mayor Joseph Smith, the city marshall and hundreds of Mormon men attack and destroy the printing press and office of *The Nauvoo Expositor*.

1844   Smith is jailed in Carthage, Illinois, on the charge of "treason" in connection with the *Expositor* incident.

1844   On June 27 a hostile mob storms the jail. Smith defends himself with a smuggled pistol, kills two men and wounds a third, but then dies in a blazing gun battle.

1846   Brigham Young leads Mormon migration from Illinois.

1847   Mormons begin settlement of Salt Lake City in a portion of Mexico soon to be ceded to the United States.

1851   Pearl of Great Price, including *Book of Abraham*, is printed.

1851   United States President Millard Fillmore appoints Brigham Young governor of Utah Territory.

1852   Mormon population of Utah numbered at 15,000.

1852   Brigham Young publicly announces plural marriage as official LDS Church policy.

1852   Conference convened at Zarahemla, Wisconsin, by disgruntled LDS Church members, the first step toward setting up the Reorganized Church of Jesus Christ of Latter Day Saints eight years later.

1857   Anti-Mormon outcries prompt President James Buchanan to send United States troops into Utah to install a non-Mormon governor.

1857   In the "Utah War" Bishop John D. Lee directs a combined force of Mormon militia and Indians in the annihilation of a wagon train on September 11, killing some 120 non-Mormon men, women, and children in the infamous Mountain Meadows Massacre.

1860   Reorganized Church of Jesus Christ of Latter Day Saints officially set up at Amboy, Illinois, with Joseph Smith III as President and Prophet.

1860   LDS Church claims 80,000 members.

1862   Congress passes Morrill Act prohibiting plural marriage.

1870   Utah grants women the right to vote.

1876   Brigham Young founds Brigham Young University.

1877   John D. Lee is executed by firing squad for his part in the Mountain Meadows Massacre.

1880   LDS Church claims 160,000 members.

1882   Federal government passes Edmunds Act with heavy penalties for polygamy; Mormon leaders are soon driven underground.

1887   Congress passes Edmunds-Tucker Act dissolving the Corporation of the Church of Jesus Christ of Latter-day Saints and seizing its property.

1890   Congress drafts legislation to disenfranchise all Mormons in the United States, whether polygamists or not.

1890   On September 25 LDS Church President Wilford Woodruff issues a Manifesto instructing Mormons to obey antipolygamy laws.

1896   Utah admitted to the Union as a state on January 4.

1900   LDS Church claims 268,000 members.

1925   LDS Church claims 613,000 members.

1947   LDS Church membership passes 1,000,000 mark.

1967   Original Egyptian papyrus from which Joseph Smith claimed to translate the Book of Abraham is rediscovered. Egyptologists translate and show it to be part of the "Book of Breathings," a funereal text not written by nor related to Abraham.

1975   LDS Church claims 3,572,000 members.

1978   An official declaration opens priesthood ordination to black men.

1978   The LDS Church reports 3,966,019 members worldwide

as of December 31, 1977, with 858,383 of these outside the United States and Canada.

1985   Ezra Taft Benson, former Eisenhower administration cabinet member, becomes the thirteenth Prophet (head) of the LDS Church.

1989   LDS Church claims 7 million members.

1989   Brigham Young University projects that LDS Church will have 265 million members by the year 2080.

1990   LDS Church reports over 43,000 full-time missionaries in the field; over 4.7 million visitors to Temple Square in Salt Lake City.

1991   LDS Church claims 8 million members.

2

What the Mormon Church Teaches

The tendency today in the Church of Jesus Christ of Latter-day Saints (also called Mormons, LDS, Mormon Church, or Mormonism) is to stress the areas of agreement with Christians rather than the areas of disagreement—especially in discussions with outsiders. And even when speaking with someone they hope to convert, Mormons realize that the newcomer is not ready to hear the deeper doctrines until a foundation has first been established. So they try to steer conversations onto common ground.

Moreover, many rank-and-file members actually remain unaware of certain teachings officially espoused by the LDS Church. In part this is due to the complex historical development of Mormon doctrine, with new publications and speeches by living prophets redefining and reinterpreting earlier thought. Also, the organization's hierarchical structure allows for beliefs to be embraced by the leadership without being communicated to the general membership or to the public. A prime example of this was the indulgence in plural marriage by Joseph Smith and his inner circle of associates while official church publications and public announcements condemned the practice. Still another reason for doctrinal ignorance on the part of many Mormons is the secretive (they call it sacred) nature of temple ceremonies. Church members who have not earned a "temple recommend" from their local leaders never get to learn the oaths, the key words, the covenants, and the secrets of the priesthood available only to temple Mormons.

All of the above factors make it unlikely that a Mormon would bring up many of the following points when asked, "What do you believe?"

Adam: Mormonism identifies Adam as Michael the Archangel prior to coming to earth and as the Ancient of days. He is expected to come again to the earth in power and glory as the patriarch of the human family before the second coming of Christ. He had flesh and bones but no blood before the fall.

Adam-God: Joseph Smith's successor, Brigham Young, taught that Adam (Eve's husband) is God—the only God worshiped by Mormons. The LDS Church leadership today publicly repudiates this doctrine, and most Mormons are unaware that Brigham Young actually taught it throughout his presidency.

Apostles: On February 14, 1835, Joseph Smith selected twelve men to fill the office of the Twelve Apostles, and successors have been appointed over the years when vacancies occurred. Mormons teach that their having "The Twelve" in their organization is one of the marks of the one true church. (The three members of the First Presidency [the President and Prophet, the top leader and his two counselors] are also apostles; therefore, they have a total of fifteen.)

Baptism: Besides the baptism of believers, the LDS Church also teaches baptism for the dead; relatives, ancestors, and others long dead can be saved by proxy baptism performed on their behalf in Mormon temples. Massive underground vaults store genealogical records involving millions of such baptisms.

Bible: Members believe the Bible to be the word of God "as far as it is translated correctly." In the Book of Mormon, 1

Nephi 13:26–29 says that "plain and precious" parts have been removed from the Bible. The uncanonized Joseph Smith Translation adds and rewrites many passages, and Mormon leaders reinterpret others in the light of alleged latter-day revelations.

Blacks: Viewing dark skin as a curse from God, Mormonism banned black men from the priesthood until a doctrinal reversal on this matter was announced in 1978.

Elohim: This is the name of God the Father, an individual distinct from Jehovah, who is the Son of Elohim.

Eternal Progression: Originally, all people existed as intelligences in the timeless past, as eternal as God himself. Then they were born into the spirit world through resurrected parents of flesh and bone. After living for a time in the spirit world, each person was eventually given a body at human birth. Our goal in this life should be to secure our resurrection as a God, in which capacity the resurrected will continue to progress, just as God did.

Exaltation: Beyond resurrection from the dead, Mormons hope to enter the highest of three heavens, the celestial kingdom, and there in the highest level of the celestial kingdom to be exalted to the status of Gods.

God(s): God the Father was once a man and still has a resurrected body of flesh and bones. Humans have the goal of becoming Gods. The basic difference between God and humans is simply that he has achieved exaltation before they have. Creation accounts in Mormon scripture speak of "the Gods" accomplishing the things Genesis says God did.

Heaven: Rather than a place where only believers go after death to be with the Lord, heaven is for virtually everyone, but consists of three distinct levels: telestial for nonbelievers, terrestrial for religious non-Mormons and backslidden Mormons, and celestial for good LDS Church members only.

Hell: The wicked go to a hell of torment, but all are eventually resurrected and pass into the telestial kingdom. Only "sons of perdition" who have given themselves over to Satan remain in hell forever.

Jehovah: This is the preincarnate name of Jesus Christ, who is one of the Gods, one of the sons of the God Elohim.

Jesus Christ: According to Mormonism Jesus Christ was one of the spirit sons of the God Elohim. Jesus was Jehovah, the God of the Old Testament. God the Father visited Mary and had marital relations with her so that Jesus could be born with a human body. Jesus redeemed all mankind to "general salvation"—secured their resurrection from the dead—but exaltation to the celestial kingdom will depend on a person's being a zealous and obedient Latter-day Saint.

Marriage: The institution of marriage is an essential cornerstone of Mormonism. Marriage partners *sealed* in a temple ceremony will be together for *time and eternity*, in this world and after death.

Michael: Michael the Archangel is the same person who was called Adam in the Garden of Eden, and who is also called the Ancient of days in the Old Testament.

Polygamy: Joseph Smith and some of his close associates practiced polygamy, starting about 1835, while publicly denying it. Later the practice was supported by alleged divine revelation and was made public. An obstacle to Utah statehood, and finally the target of a federal law enforcement crackdown, plural marriage was officially discontinued in 1890.

Salvation: Because of Christ's atonement everyone will partake of what Mormons call unconditional or general salvation, resurrection from the dead. Conditional or individual salvation involves entering the celestial kingdom and is a complex matter depending on such things as membership in the LDS Church, obedience to its ordinances, and so on. Even beyond this is full salvation, available only to faithful Mormons who have gone through temple ceremonies; those who obtain it are exalted and become Gods.

Temple: While local Mormon Church buildings, called chapels, are viewed in much the same way as Christians view theirs, the large Mormon temples are accorded special status. Temple ceremonies are off limits to nonmembers and even to Mormons who do not possess a "temple recommend" from their leaders. These ceremonies include celestial marriage, baptism for the dead, endowments, and other sacred rites.

Women: Barred from the priesthood and from the LDS hierarchy, women depend on men even for their heavenly exaltation. Without a Mormon husband in good standing, a Mormon woman has no hope of exaltation to the level of Goddess; nor can a man become a God without a faithful Mormon wife. But, if their marriages are sealed in temple ceremonies, women may continue to have spirit children throughout eternity.

3

Mormon Scripture

---

he Church of Jesus Christ of Latter-day Saints refers
to four volumes as the *standard works* of the church,
its canonized scripture: The Holy Bible (King James
Version), Book of Mormon, Doctrine and
Covenants, and Pearl of Great Price. All four are considered to
be the word of God, and one would expect them to be in perfect
harmony with one another. In actuality, though, there is a great
deal of doctrinal contradiction among them. Current Mormon
doctrine can best be discerned from other sources such as talks by
top church leaders at official functions, LDS teaching manuals,
church magazines and newspapers, and books written by top LDS
leaders through the Deseret Book Company in Salt Lake City.
Since the top official of the church is viewed as the living
Prophet, with authority to speak for God, it is understandable
that doctrine will vary over the years, with the utterances of the
current Prophet reinterpreting and overruling some earlier teachings. Bearing this in mind, we here present a brief overview of the
Mormon *standard works*.

The Bible

In "The Articles of Faith" Joseph Smith wrote: "We believe
the Bible to be the word of God as far as it is translated correctly;

we also believe the Book of Mormon to be the word of God."
(1:8, Pearl of Great Price, 1971 edition, p. 59). But Mormons
believe the Bible to be incomplete, because the Book of Mormon
states that "many parts" of the Bible are missing (1 Nephi
13:26–29). The implication of all this is that the Book of
Mormon is more reliable than the Bible, and in fact Mormons do
rely on it and stress it as sacred Scripture more so than the Bible.

LDS Church leaders have acknowledged that their teachings
are not derived primarily from the Bible, but that they use the
Bible in persuading others to believe. Thus LeGrand Richards,
one of the "general authorities" of the church, concludes a doctrinal discussion in his book A Marvelous Work And A Wonder by
saying: "The knowledge of all these things, as the reader will note,
does not come to us primarily through reading the Bible, but
through the revelations of the Lord in these latter days. We use
the Bible to show that these teachings are completely in accord
therewith" (1979 edition, p. 128).

The LDS Church publishes for the use of its members a King
James Bible complete with a topical guide, a Bible dictionary, and
extensive footnotes cross referencing Mormon writings. Included
in the footnotes and in the Appendix are excerpts from the Joseph
Smith Translation (JST), not actually a fresh translation but a revision of the King James Version, supposedly correcting errors, addi-
tions, and deletions that had crept into the text over the years.
Joseph Smith made his "corrections" throughout the Bible, not
by consulting ancient manuscripts but allegedly by receiving
divine inspiration. Strangely, though, the LDS Church has not
formally canonized Smith's variations by including them in the
text as sacred Scripture, but it has given them official sanction by
including some of them in the footnotes and appendix of their
King James Bible. They have never published the complete
"translation."

Smith's wife Emma refused to give the manuscript of the Joseph
Smith Translation to Brigham Young, but in 1866 she presented it
to the Reorganized Church of Jesus Christ of Latter Day Saints
(RLDS), and that breakaway group published it the following
year. In 1974 the LDS Church finally obtained microfilm copies
of the manuscript from the RLDS Church but has continued to

hold back from publishing it, although the edition published by the RLDS Church is available at the LDS Deseret Book Store in Salt Lake City, where Mormons freely purchase it.

The *Joseph Smith Translation* apparently puts the Mormon leadership in somewhat of a dilemma. Some of Smith's revisions to the King James text fail to agree with the same passages as quoted in the Book of Mormon. Other portions contradict current Mormon doctrine. Therefore, fully endorsing it could prove embarrassing, but flatly rejecting it as erroneous would discredit Smith as a prophet. Instead, LDS leaders have sidestepped the issue by alleging that the work Smith began in 1831 was left unfinished at his untimely death in 1844: numerous errors remain in the uncorrected portions of the King James text, and therefore publication would be inappropriate. However, in a letter Smith wrote dated July 2, 1833 at Kirtland, Ohio, he states that he "this day finished the translating of the Scriptures" (History of the Church, vol. 1, p. 368).

In any case, Mormons today do use the King James Version Bible in discussions with Christians, citing Scripture in support of LDS Church doctrines. In the verse-by-verse sections of this book we demonstrate that those citations do not in fact support Mormon doctrine, but rather that the Bible discredits both the doctrine and the other alleged scriptures of the LDS Church.

Book of Mormon

Some eight million members of the Church of Jesus Christ of Latter-day Saints regard the Book of Mormon as a volume of Holy Scripture comparable to the Bible. They accept it as an inspired record of God's dealings with the inhabitants of the Americas, just as the Bible records his dealings with the Jews. Because the Book of Mormon includes accounts of alleged visits to America by the resurrected Christ, it contains elements similar to both the Old and New Testaments of the Bible. Current editions include a subtitle, so that the volume is fully titled The Book of Mormon: Another Testament of Jesus Christ. This should call to mind the Bible's warning: "But though we, or an angel from heaven, preach

any other gospel unto you than that which we have preached
unto you, let him be accursed" (Gal. 1:8).

First published in 1830 in Palmyra, New York, the original edition says on its title page: "by Joseph Smith, Junior, author and
proprietor." Current editions say: "translated by Joseph Smith,
Jun."

Smith claimed that he was visited on September 21, 1823, by
the angel Moroni, resurrected son of an ancient prophet-historian
named Mormon who had written on gold plates quotations and
abridgements of earlier writers Nephi, Jacob, Enos, et al. Before
dying as the last of the Nephite people in A.D. 421, Moroni buried
the golden plates in a stone vault on the Hill Cumorah between
Palmyra and Manchester in western New York State. The angel
took young Smith to the site in 1823 and let him unearth the
stone vault and look into it, but did not allow him to remove the
gold plates until 1827. Then, along with the plates, Smith
retrieved from the vault the Urim and Thummim, two stones set
in silver bows, like eyeglasses, which enabled him miraculously to
translate the "reformed Egyptian" characters written on the
plates. After the translation work was completed the angel
Moroni reappeared and took back the plates.

Unlike the books and epistles of the Bible that are attested to
by thousands of ancient manuscripts such as the Dead Sea Scrolls,
which have been unearthed and preserved for inspection today,
the 1830 Book of Mormon exists only as an English-language
"translation" by one Joseph Smith. And aside from the fact that
his account of the angel and the golden plates is difficult for many
to believe, there are other reasons for questioning the authenticity
of the Book of Mormon.

One reason is Joseph Smith's personal background. Numerous
reports from the period allege that he was a con man with a history of using a "peep stone" he put in his hat and then claimed it
showed him where his clients might be successful in "money digging" or treasure hunting. Mormons respond that these charges
surfaced when disgruntled former members of the church began
seeking ways to attack him. But public records establish that
Joseph was brought to trial for such activities in Bainbridge, New
York, on March 20, 1826—four years before he set up his church

and six years after he claimed to have been visited by God the Father and Jesus Christ. Official documents refer to him as "Joseph Smith The Glass Looker," because it was an agate-like stone he used as a crystal ball to dupe people.

Another problem revolves around allegations that Smith took much of the Book of Mormon from an unpublished novel titled *Manuscript Found*[1] by retired Congregational minister Solomon Spalding (1761–1816). Affidavits to that effect by Spalding's widow, relatives, and neighbors were published in book form as *Mormonism Unvailed* by Eber D. Howe in 1834. Other material in the Book of Mormon closely parallels portions of *View of the Hebrews* by Ethan Smith (Poultney, Vermont, 1825). Ethan Smith was the Cowdery family's pastor in Poultney, Vermont, at the time Oliver Cowdery, Smith's scribe, left there in 1825. It is possible that Oliver had a copy of *View of the Hebrews*.

Although books have been and, no doubt, will continue to be written on the origin of the Book of Mormon, our verse-by-verse section of this book devoted to it will focus on internal evidence rather than such historical evidence. The contents of the Book of Mormon will be shown not only to contradict current teaching of the LDS Church but also to contradict the Bible, historical fact, and common sense.

LDS Apostle LeGrand Richards reports that Brigham Young's close associate Dr. Willard Richards made this remark after reading from the Book of Mormon for the first time: "That book was either written by God or the devil, and I am going to find out who wrote it."[2] Ten days later he concluded that it was from God. Many informed readers, however, have reached a different conclusion.

Doctrine and Covenants

Joseph Smith's first sixty-five "revelations" were published in 1833 as the *Book of Commandments for the Government of the Church of Christ*. This was revised and expanded in 1835 as the Doctrine and Covenants of the Church of the Latter Day Saints.[3] Today's version, 1990 printing, contains 138 Sections plus 2

Official Declarations. Most of the sections are introduced as revelations given to Joseph Smith. Significant exceptions are Section
135, which contains the official version of Smith's "martyrdom,"
and Section 136, presented as "The Word and Will of the Lord,
given through President Brigham Young." Sections 137 (Smith's
"Vision of the Celestial Kingdom") and 138 (twentieth-century
leader Joseph F. Smith's "Vision of the Redemption of the Dead")
were officially added in 1979.

Unlike the much larger Book of Mormon which consists
mostly of purported history but provides little in the way of
unique LDS Church doctrine, Doctrine and Covenants is full of
instructions for the church as to belief and practice. Concepts
such as baptism for the dead, celestial marriage, priesthood, and
polygamy are introduced and elaborated upon. At the end of the
138 sections is a brief Official Declaration from LDS Church
President Wilford Woodruff ending polygamous marriage in 1890,
and the 1978 Official Declaration allowing black men to hold the
priesthood.

Pearl of Great Price

This Mormon *standard work*, roughly sixty pages long in recent
printings, is actually a collection of smaller writings: the *Book of
Moses*, the *Book of Abraham*, portions from Joseph Smith's revision of Matthew's Gospel, Smith's account of his early visions and
the golden plates, and the brief Mormon "Articles of Faith."

The *Book of Moses* is an elaboration and rewriting of the Book
of Genesis. Copying much from the King James Version, it also
adds some unique Mormon teachings. For example, it has Satan
saying, "Behold, here I am, send me, I will be thy son, and I will
redeem all mankind, that one soul shall not be lost, and surely I
will do it" (Moses 4:1). And the doctrine of spirit pre-existence
before human birth is inserted: "And I, the Lord God, had created all the children of men; and not yet a man to till the ground;
for in heaven created I them; and there was not yet flesh upon
the earth. . . . I made the world, and men before they were in the
flesh" (Moses 3:5; 6:51). Moreover, Eve is made to say, "Were it
not for our transgression, we should never have had seed," thus

claiming disobedience to have been necessary for human procreation (Moses 5:11). And Adam goes on to be baptized in water and to be "born of the Spirit" (Moses 6:64, 65).

The *Book of Abraham* is unique in that it features three cuts or facsimiles of the Egyptian papyrus from which Joseph Smith claimed he "translated" it, with numbers keying the Egyptian symbols to explanatory notes below each cut. It is described as "The writings of Abraham while he was in Egypt, called the *Book of Abraham*, written by his own hand, upon papyrus."

This papyrus actually exists, having been seen in Smith's possession, along with Egyptian mummies, by reputable non-Mormon visitors. But Smith's "translation" had to be miraculous, since he possessed no academic training in linguistics, and even trained Egyptologists were just beginning to discover how to decode hieroglyphic writing in his day. After being lost for some years and presumed destroyed, the papyrus was found in 1967 in New York's Metropolitan Museum and identified by museum scholars and Mormon leaders as the same from which Smith had "translated" the *Book of Abraham*. It was examined and translated by experts, both Mormon and non-Mormon, in the now fully developed field of Egyptian hieroglyphics, with all of them concluding that the writings formed part of the "Book of Breathings," a pagan Egyptian funereal text totally unrelated to Abraham, and that the correct translation bore no resemblance whatsoever to Joseph Smith's *Book of Abraham*.

In 1978, about a dozen years after this major embarrassment, the LDS Church issued an Official Declaration dropping its long-standing ban on black men in the priesthood, but did not mention that the ban had been based largely on the now academically discredited *Book of Abraham* (1:21–26). Still, the book remains part of Mormon sacred scripture and a basis for other unique beliefs. It teaches, for example, the plurality of Gods: "And they went down at the beginning, and they, that is the Gods, organized and formed the heavens and the earth" (Abraham 4:1). And it provides the basis for belief that these gods came from the star Kolob to do their creative work in this part of the universe (Abraham 3:3, 9).

The heading under *Joseph Smith—Matthew* says: "An extract from the translation of the Bible as revealed to Joseph Smith the Prophet in 1831: Matthew 23:39 and chapter 24."

This part of the Pearl of Great Price covers slightly more than three pages and has fifty-five verses. The "translation of the Bible" mentioned is called the *Joseph Smith Translation* (JST) in the appendix of the Holy Bible published by the Church of Jesus Christ of Latter-day Saints, Salt Lake City, 1979. There is additional information on this translation under "The Bible" in our chapter 3.

Joseph Smith—Matthew is essentially the same as the Inspired Version, Matthew 23:39–41, 24:1–56, in *Joseph Smith's New Translation of the Bible* (Herald Publishing House, 1970). The wording and punctuation is slightly different and the verses are numbered differently. Herald is the publishing arm of the Reorganized Church of Jesus Christ of Latter Day Saints, Independence, Missouri, which owns the original Joseph Smith manuscripts.

The heading under *Joseph Smith—History* says: "Extracts from the History of Joseph Smith, the Prophet, History of the Church, Vol. 1, Chapters 1–5."

It covers thirteen pages in seventy-five verses and footnotes. In it the founder of the Mormon Church, Joseph Smith, tells about his alleged firsthand experiences in the beginning of the Mormon Church. Major events include: the First Vision story, the visits of the angel Moroni, the receiving of and translation of the golden plates, Martin Harris's trip to New York City with a transcript of the reformed Egyptian characters from the Book of Mormon to Professor Charles Anthon and Dr. Samuel Latham Mitchill, the receiving of the Aaronic Priesthood, the baptism of Joseph Smith and his scribe, Oliver Cowdery.

"The Articles of Faith of the Church of Jesus Christ of Latter-day Saints, *History of the Church*, Vol. 4, pp. 535-541," covers less than two pages in thirteen verses and footnotes. The original was written in 1842, by Joseph Smith in a letter to John Wentworth of the *Chicago Democrat*. Untitled and unnumbered then, with no footnotes, the thirteen articles had essentially the same wording as the present ones do.

Mormon missionaries hand out the Articles of Faith as a summary of the beliefs of the Mormon Church. The knowledgeable reader will note that much is left out or glossed over; the Articles of Faith do not represent real Mormon doctrine.

These should not be confused with the book *Articles of Faith* by James Talmage, which is an expansion of the brief creedal statements and does represent real Mormon doctrine.

4

Verse-by-Verse Answers for Mormons: Old Testament

Genesis

Genesis 1:26, 27

And God said, Let us make man in our image. . . . So God created man in his own image, in the image of God created he him; male and female created he them.

The Mormon Church uses these verses to support two of its distinctive teachings: (1) that God has a body resembling our own, and (2) that the Trinity actually consists of three separate and distinct Gods who are one only in purpose.

To derive the first idea, the "image of God" referred to here is interpreted as a physical image, so the verses are understood to mean that man is in the physical likeness of God, with the converse also being true, namely, that God has a humanlike body of flesh and bones with essentially human proportions.

Christians, on the other hand, generally understand God's image as referring to the divine moral and intellectual qualities imparted to man, rather than physical resemblance. The beasts of the earth created in verses 24 and 25 evidently include gorillas and apes with bodies similar to ours and with eyes, nose, and mouth arranged much as they are on a human face. The striking difference about man created in verse 26 is not so much physical as spiritual. Unlike the beasts, man was made with a view toward the day when "we all, with open face beholding as in a glass the glory of the Lord, are changed into the same image from glory to glory, even as by the Spirit of the Lord" (2 Cor. 3:18).

As to man's physical form, if it were truly the same as God's there would have been no need for Christ to change his form when he came to earth as described in Philippians 2:6, 7: "Who, being in the form of God, thought it not robbery to be equal with God: but made himself of no reputation, and took upon him the form of a servant, and was made in the likeness of men." The fact that Christ had to give up "being in the form of God" to be "made in the likeness of men" shows that the two are not the same.

This does not mean, of course, that God has a body grotesquely different from our own, but, rather, what we read in Scripture teaches us that God is of an entirely different form altogether: while man is mere flesh and blood, "God is a Spirit" (John 4:24 KJV) or "God is Spirit," (NIV, RSV).

See also the discussions of Genesis 32:30, Exodus 33:11, and Hebrews 1:3.

Before going on to the second issue a word should be said about what Christians can hope to accomplish through discussions such as the above. While you may be able to answer Mormon misinterpretation of a particular Bible verse, you should not expect to convince your Mormon listener that his belief is wrong, at least not immediately. The reason for this is that the Mormon's belief is not really based on that Bible verse, but rather on the official teachings of the LDS Church. He may now realize that the verse in question does not support his belief, but that is not a big problem for him, because his belief rests solidly, he thinks, on other support. For example, in the case just discussed it does not matter to the Mormon that Genesis 1:26 does not say God has a body like ours, because that belief of his is actually based on what he reads in works such as *Teachings of the Prophet Joseph Smith* by Joseph Fielding Smith (Deseret Book Company, 1976, p. 345):

God himself was once as we are now, and is an exalted man, and sits enthroned in yonder heavens! . . . If you were to see him today, you would see him like a man in form—like yourselves in all the person, image, and very form as a man; for Adam was created in the very fashion, image and likeness of God.

Resting his faith on such writings of his church rather than on the Bible, the Mormon will not see the need to change his beliefs until confronted with overwhelming evidence that the LDS Church is not to be relied on for sound religious teaching. Christians engaging in discussions with Mormons need to realize this to avoid disappointment and discouragement.

As to God's saying "Let *us* make man in *our* image," orthodox Christians offer more than one possible explanation for the use of plural pronouns. But the use of the plural in no way conflicts with the orthodox doctrine of the Trinity, nor does it support the Mormon view that the Trinity consists of three separate and distinct Gods who are *One* only in purpose.[1] Although LDS missionaries may cite Genesis 1:26, 27 in support of this view, Christians should be aware that the Mormons are really deriving their theology from another source that they would prefer not to reveal to you, namely, Pearl of Great Price, which they accept as scripture. In the portion of this work known as *The Book of Abraham* the plural form Gods takes the place of the singular God: "And the Gods took counsel among themselves and said: Let us go down and form man in our image, after our likeness. . . . So the Gods went down to organize man in their own image, in the image of the Gods to form they him, male and female to form they them" (Abraham 4:26, 27).

The polytheistic interpretation of Genesis 1:26–27 does not rest on the words found in the Bible. Although they may argue that it does, in their own minds the Mormons are really thinking of the wording they are accustomed to in their *Book of Abraham*. That is the real foundation of their polytheistic belief. But how firm a foundation is it? The ancient Egyptian papyrus that Joseph Smith called *The Book of Abraham* was examined in 1967 and 1968 by both Mormon and non-Mormon Egyptologists, and they found the actual meaning of the hieroglyphic writings to be totally different from Prophet Smith's "translation." The words that Mormons trust as a foundation for their beliefs are simply not there in the original. (For more information on *Book of Abraham* see the discussion in chapter 3, "Mormon Scripture.")

In contrast to the discredited *Book of Abraham*, the Bible's Genesis account is supported by hundreds of ancient manuscripts, all confirming the words quoted above. But what do those words mean? Some Christians explain that God is speaking in Genesis 1:26, 27 as divine King in his heavenly court, and so the use of *us* and *our* is simply the "plural of majesty," a form of speech in which a king or a queen traditionally says *we* rather than *I*. An example of this is found in the oft-quoted words of Britain's Queen Victoria when she saw an imitation of herself by Alexander Grantham Yorke. The Queen responded, "We are not amused." Certainly no one would argue from this that Victoria consisted of three separate and distinct persons; no, she was merely using the plural of majesty. Similarly, then, Almighty God—the most majestic ruler in all the universe—would be entitled to use the plural of majesty recorded in Genesis 1:26, 27.

Another possibility is that God was here speaking to the angelic spirit creatures in his court, including them in the word *we*, since they, too, had been created in his image and shared that image. Created "a little lower than the angels" (Ps. 8:5), man would be made in that same image that the angels received from God so that he, in speaking to the angels, could call it *our* image.

But even if the plural is used because God the Father is speaking to God the Son, as some Christians believe, this still does not disprove the Christian doctrine of the Trinity. In the Trinity the Father may speak to the Son, and vice versa. Many Mormons mistakenly think Christians believe in modalism—one person appearing in three modes—but the orthodox statement of the doctrine is that the Father, the Son, and the Holy Spirit are *three* persons who are of the same divine nature, thus one God. So, it is no problem for Christians that the Father speaks to the Son here, or that the Son prays to the Father in John chapter 17.

See also the discussion of Matthew 3:16, 17.

Genesis 2:7

And the Lord God formed man of the dust of the ground, and breathed into his nostrils the breath of life; and man became a living soul.

The apostle Paul adds his testimony to the truthfulness of the Genesis account of creation: "And so it is written, The first man Adam was made a living soul. . . . The first man is of the earth, earthy" (1 Cor. 15:45, 47). But Brigham Young, second President and Prophet of the Mormon Church denies it, flatly contradicting the Bible:

> Though we have it in history that our father Adam was made of the dust of this earth, and that he knew nothing about his God previous to being made here, yet it is not so; and when we learn the truth we shall see and understand that he helped to make this world, and was the chief manager in that operation.
> He was the person who brought the animals and the seeds from other planets to this world, and brought a wife with him and stayed here. You may read and believe what you please as to what is found written in the Bible. Adam was made from the dust of an earth, but not from the dust of this earth. (Brigham Young, *Journal of Discourses*, vol. 3, p. 319).

In these few words Brigham Young not only (1) denies the Bible's inspired account of Adam's creation, but also (2) says Adam "brought a wife with him" to this planet, thus contradicting what Genesis 2:22 says about Eve, (3) says Adam "brought the animals and the seeds from other planets," thus negating more of the Genesis account, and (4) places Adam as "the chief manager" in the creation of the world.

Well, then, just who did Brigham Young believe Adam to be, if Adam created this world? The answer is found in another of the sermons this Mormon Prophet gave in his official capacity as God's spokesman to the Church of Jesus Christ of Latter-day Saints:

> When our father Adam came into the garden of Eden, he came into it with a celestial body, and brought Eve, one of his wives, with him. He helped to make and organize this world. He is MICHAEL, the Archangel, the ANCIENT OF DAYS! about whom holy men have written and spoken—He is our FATHER and our GOD, and the only God with whom WE have to do.

—(*The Latter-Day Saints' MILLENNIAL STAR*, vol. XV, no. 48, Saturday, November 26, 1853, quoting from Brigham Young, *Journal of Discourses*, vol. 1, pp. 50, 51).

Yes, unbelievable as it may seem, Brigham Young taught that Adam is God, "the only God with whom we have to do." Other Mormon leaders joined him in proclaiming the same thing: "I have learned by experience that there is but one God that pertains to this people, and He is the God that pertains to this earth—the first man. That first man sent his own Son to redeem the world." (Heber C. Kimball, *Journal of Discourses*, 1856, vol. 4, p. 1).

In fairness to modern-day Mormons, it should be said that most of them neither know of nor believe in the Adam-God doctrine. Although Brigham Young persisted in teaching it for more than twenty years, his successors at the head of the LDS Church have done their best to cover up that fact, pushing Adam-God under the rug, so to speak. It has not been taught since the turn of the century, and in 1976 the twelfth President, Spencer Kimball, strongly denounced the doctrine. Still, when pressed, some Mormons may admit that the "God" they worship is "the God of this planet," that this God was a man before he became God, and that they, too, hope someday to become "Gods" of their own planets. Moreover, the Bible Dictionary at the back of the Mormon Bible (1990 printing) concludes its article under the heading "God" by saying, "Latter-day revelation confirms the biblical account of God as the literal father of the human family" (p. 682).

For further consideration of the Adam-God doctrine see the discussion of Daniel 7:9, 13, 22.

Genesis 11:7

Go to, let us go down, and there confound their language, that they may not understand one another's speech.

Mormons see the use of the plural pronoun *us* as support for their belief in the plurality of Gods. See the discussion of the similar expression in Genesis 1:26, 27.

Genesis 11:8, 9

So the LORD scattered them abroad from thence upon the face of all the earth: and they left off to build the city. Therefore is the name of it called Babel; because the LORD did there confound the language of all the earth: and from thence did the LORD scatter them abroad upon the face of all the earth.

Mormons may use this passage to introduce a discussion of the alleged history of ancient America contained in the Book of Mormon. They have been taught that one of the evidences of "divine authenticity" of the Book of Mormon is that it provides the history of the early inhabitants of America. The earliest of these, according to the Book of Mormon, were the Jaredites, whose story begins with the tower of Babel. (See the discussion of Ether 1:33–37 in chapter 6.)

Genesis 14:18

And Melchizedek king of Salem brought forth bread and wine: and he was the priest of the most high God.

Mormons claim to be the modern successors to Melchizedek's priesthood. But the Bible reveals that the prophecy of a priesthood patterned after that of Melchizedek finds its fulfillment in the person of Jesus Christ, and that Christ has this priesthood without successor; it is not transferable. There is no evidence, biblical or otherwise, that Jesus Christ passed on this priesthood to anyone. In fact, Hebrews 7:23 explains that the Jews had many priests over the years because each one eventually died and had to be succeeded by another, whereas (v. 24), "this man [Jesus], because he continueth ever, hath an unchangeable priesthood," or "a priesthood that needs no successor" (*Phillips*).

Moreover, for this reason we today do not need to become priests ourselves, or to have human priests perform services on our behalf; Jesus Christ is the only priest we need. Because he is a priest forever, after the order of Melchizedek, "he is able to save them to the uttermost that come unto God by him, seeing he ever liveth to make intercession for them" (Heb. 7:25).

See also Psalm 110:4; Hebrews 5:6; and the discussion of Acts 3:20, 21.

Genesis 32:30

And Jacob called the name of the place Peniel: for I have seen God face to face, and my life is preserved.

This is a verse used by Mormons to support their teaching that God has a body. The context reveals that Jacob said the above after a wrestling match: "And Jacob was left alone; and there wrestled a man with him until the breaking of the day" (v. 24). It was this "man" that Jacob actually saw "face to face." Who was this "man"? Was he God, as the Mormons would have us believe?

Again, the context provides the answer. This chapter of Genesis begins by saying, "And Jacob went on his way, and the angels of God met him" (v. 1). Seeing an angelic representative of God face to face was, in effect, a personal encounter with God. Inspired writings elsewhere in the Bible confirm that it was an angel who wrestled with Jacob, rather than God himself: "Yea, he had power over the angel" (Hos. 12:4).

See also the discussions of Genesis 1:26, 27; Exodus 24:10, 11; 33:11, 22; Deuteronomy 4:28; and John 1:18.

Genesis 37:5, 10

And Joseph dreamed a dream, and he told it his brethren: and they hated him yet the more. . . . And he told it to his father, and to his brethren: and his father rebuked him, and said unto him, What is this dream that thou hast dreamed? Shall I and thy mother and thy brethren indeed come to bow down ourselves to thee to the earth?

Mormons may read the grand promises given to Joseph in his prophetic dreams and ask, "Where does the Bible record the fulfillment of these wonderful promises on Joseph's descendants?" The answer, they suggest, is that the Bible does not record the fulfillment at all, but rather God inspired the Book of Mormon to preserve the history of a branch of the house of Joseph that migrated to ancient America. Thus they believe the Bible is shown to be incomplete without the Book of Mormon.

But there is a major fallacy in this argument. By directing their listeners' gaze far afield in search of a fulfillment of Joseph's prophetic dreams, the Mormons are missing the actual fulfillment that is recorded in the Book of Genesis a few chapters later:

Sold into slavery by his brothers, Joseph was taken to Egypt where he eventually became the second-most-powerful man in the country, next to Pharaoh himself. Then a famine forced his brothers to come to Egypt looking for food. Not recognizing Joseph in his Egyptian garb and in his role as governor, "Joseph's brethren came, and bowed down themselves before him with their faces to the earth. . . . And Joseph remembered the dreams which he had dreamed of them" (Gen. 42:6, 9). This is the fulfillment. Just as Joseph had dreamed, his brothers came and bowed down before him. Since the fulfillment is not missing but is recorded in Genesis, there is no need to look outside the Bible. Joseph's prophetic dreams provide no justification for the Book of Mormon.

For more about the Mormon claim that Israelites inhabited ancient America see the discussions of Matthew 15:24; John 10:16; and 3 Nephi 15:17, 21, 22.

Exodus

Exodus 6:3

And I appeared unto Abraham, unto Isaac, and unto Jacob, by the name of God Almighty, but by my name JEHOVAH was I not known to them.

Unlike many pseudo-Christian cults that deny the deity of Christ, the Mormon Church teaches that Jesus Christ is Jehovah (the LORD) of the Old Testament. Mormons may even properly associate Old Testament verses with New Testament verses to show that Jesus is Jehovah: Deuteronomy 1:32, 33 with 1 Corinthians 10:1–4; Isaiah 43:3, 11 with Luke 2:11; and Isaiah 48:17 with Romans 3:24. If the discussion goes only this far, a Christian may assume that his Mormon acquaintance agrees with him theologically. But that is not actually the case. While the Christian understands Jehovah to be one of the Hebrew names of the triune deity—Father, Son, and Holy Spirit—the Mormon believes quite differently. His church's Bible Dictionary (Salt Lake City, 1990 printing, p. 681) explains it this way:

> When one speaks of God, it is generally the Father who is referred to; that is, Elohim. All mankind are his children. The personage known as Jehovah in Old Testament times, and who is usually identified in the Old Testament as LORD (in capital letters), is the Son, known as Jesus Christ, and who is also a God . . . he being the eldest of the spirit children of Elohim. . . . The Holy Ghost is also a God.

The Mormon sees the Father, Son, and Holy Spirit as three Gods who are merely "unified in purpose."[2] While Christians understand *Elohim* and *Jehovah* to be names belonging to the one true God of the Bible, Mormons believe that each of these names designates a different God.

This view, however, that Elohim and Jehovah are distinct individuals can be maintained only when reading a Bible that substitutes the less specific words *God* and LORD. Examination of the Hebrew text immediately shows that Elohim and Jehovah are one and the same. For example, throughout Genesis chapter 2 wherever "the LORD God" is spoken of, this is "Jehovah Elohim" in Hebrew. When Jacob says to Isaac, "Because the LORD thy God brought it to me," the literal reading is, "Because Jehovah thy Elohim brought it to me" (Gen. 27:20). When the LORD (Jehovah) speaks to Moses at the burning bush, he introduces himself by saying, "I am the God [*Elohim* in Hebrew] of thy father, the God of Abraham, the God of Isaac, and the God of Jacob. . . . And the LORD [Jehovah in Hebrew] said . . . " (Exod. 3:6, 7).

See also the discussion of Deuteronomy 6:4.

Exodus 24:10, 11

And they saw the God of Israel: and there was under his feet as it were a paved work of a sapphire stone, and as it were the body of heaven in his clearness. And upon the nobles of the children of Israel he laid not his hand: also they saw God, and did eat and drink.

Does God actually have hands and feet, a human body? Mormonism teaches that he does, and Mormons turn to passages such as this to support that belief. But when Moses and his associates "saw God," was it in a literal sense, or in the visionary sense in which prophets were allowed to "see" future events? God later told Moses that "there shall no man see me, and live" (Exod. 33:20). And the New Testament asserts that "no man hath seen God at any time; the only begotten Son, which is in the bosom of the Father, he hath declared him" (John 1:18).

For more on this matter see the discussions of Genesis 1:16, 27; 32:30; Exodus 33:11; and John 1:18.

Exodus 33:11

And the LORD spake unto Moses face to face, as a man speaketh unto his friend.

This verse is cited by Mormons in their attempt to prove that God the Father is a man who achieved godhood and who still has a humanlike body, the body in which he allegedly appeared to Joseph Smith.

However, the context says that "as Moses entered into the tabernacle, the cloudy pillar descended, and stood at the door of the tabernacle, and the LORD talked with Moses" (v. 9). God spoke to Moses from within the pillar of cloud, which served as a visible reminder of his presence. This repeated the pattern of Moses' first conversation with God at the burning bush. On that occasion "God called unto him out of the midst of the bush, and said, Moses, Moses" (Exod. 3:4). As on later occasions the face-to-face aspect of the conversation was not that Moses necessarily saw a literal face before his eyes but that he had a two-way, give-and-take conversation with God.[3]

The Lord himself explained it this way when Miriam and Aaron challenged the authority of their fleshly brother Moses: "If there be a prophet among you, I the LORD will make myself known unto him in a vision, and will speak unto him in a dream. My servant Moses is not so, who is faithful in all mine house. With him I speak mouth to mouth, even apparently, and not in dark speeches; and the similitude of the LORD shall he behold"

(Num. 12:6–8). In contrast to other prophets who would hear from God through dreams or visions, Moses was privileged to have back-and-forth dialogue with God, fully conscious and awake, just as a man would converse with his friend.

Did Moses actually see God's face during these encounters? The answer is stated plainly in the immediate context. In Exodus 33:20, God told Moses, "Thou canst not see my face: for there shall no man see me, and live."

Then he put Moses on a rock, saying, "And it shall come to pass, while my glory passeth by, that I will put thee in a clift of the rock, and will cover thee with my hand while I pass by; And I will take away mine hand, and thou shalt see my back parts: but my face shall not be seen" (vv. 22, 23). God's "hand" would cover Moses and shield him as God passed by. But a man's literal hand would be nowhere near large enough to cover Moses and afford him this protection. Nor could a man's hand remain in place while he passed by. These facts indicate that God's references to his face, hand, and back parts amounted to figurative language; he was not speaking literally in describing himself.

The statement that "the LORD spake unto Moses face to face" provides no basis at all for the Mormon argument that God the Father has a man's face and body. Rather, the Bible tells us, "God is a Spirit," and therefore, "no man hath seen God at any time" (John 1:18).

See also the discussions of Genesis 1:26, 27; 32:30; Exodus 24:10, 11; Deuteronomy 4:28; and John 1:18.

Deuteronomy

Deuteronomy 4:2
Ye shall not add unto the word which I command you, neither shall ye diminish ought from it, that ye may keep the commandments of the LORD your God which I command you.

Revelation 22:18 warns: "For I testify unto every man that heareth the words of the prophecy of this book, If any man shall add unto these things, God shall add unto him the plagues that are written in this book." When shown that verse by Christians objecting to the Book of Mormon, members of the LDS Church will often respond by turning to Deuteronomy 4:2 and say that if Revelation 22:18 rules out the Book of Mormon, Deuteronomy 4:2 rules out the remaining sixty-one books of the Bible that come after it.

However, these words in Deuteronomy do not rule out additional revelation from God; they simply forbid *men* from adding anything on their own to what God has inspired. When the command came from God to Jeremiah the prophet, saying, "Thus speaketh the LORD God of Israel, saying, Write thee all the words that I have spoken unto thee in a book" (Jer. 30:2), it was proper for Jeremiah to comply. What would have been wrong would have been for Jeremiah to add on his own to what the LORD told him to write.

To see how this applies to the Book of Mormon and other latter-day scriptures of the LDS Church, see chapter 3, "Mormon Scripture," and chapter 6, "Verse-by-Verse Answers for Mormons— Book of Mormon." See also the discussion of Revelation 22:18.

Deuteronomy 4:28

And there ye shall serve gods, the work of men's hands, wood and stone, which neither see, nor hear, nor eat, nor smell.

Centuries after Moses recorded this prophecy, the nation of Israel was carried off captive to lands where people worshiped idols—gods of wood and stone. But some Mormons believe this verse applies also to the Catholic and Protestant churches. They believe that strange Gods of christendom are worshiped in those churches, "gods made by the hands of man"—by church leaders who apostatized from the true faith and invented a counterfeit theology (*A Marvelous Work And A Wonder*, by Mormon Apostle LeGrand Richards, 1979 edition, p. 12). "The false gods of Christendom bear the same names as the true Gods of the Bible. Beyond this they have little resemblance" (*A New Witness for the Articles of Faith*, by Bruce R. McConkie, p.55).

The true God, according to Mormonism, is a former man who still has a humanlike body and who can therefore see, hear, eat, and smell with his eyes, ears, mouth, and nose. Anyone worshiping a God who is a spirit and therefore lacks those literal human body parts falls into the same category as the idolaters described in Deuteronomy, in the Mormon's view. They charge Catholics and Protestants with worshiping a God who can "neither see, nor hear, nor eat, nor smell."

Yet, God declares in the Bible, "I am God, and not man" (Hos. 11:9). Since "in the beginning God created the heaven and the earth" and said, "Let there be light: and there was light," it should be obvious that he could see that light even before he formed any creatures having eyes (Gen. 1:1, 3). As the psalmist puts it, "He that planted the ear, shall he not hear? he that formed the eye, shall he not see?" (Ps. 94:9).

No, the God Christians worship is not "the work of men's hands" (Deut. 4:28). Nor is he a former man, like the gods of Mormonism. Rather, the true God is "from everlasting to everlasting" (Ps. 106:48; 41:13). And, far from having the proportions of a man, he is so great that King Solomon prayed, "But will God indeed dwell on the earth? behold, the heaven and heaven of heavens cannot contain thee; how much less this house that I have builded?" (1 Kings 8:27).

For further refutation of the LDS claim that God the Father has a resurrected body of flesh and bones, see the discussions of Genesis 1:26, 27; 32:30; Exodus 24:10, 11; 33:11.

Deuteronomy 6:4

Hear, O Israel: The LORD our God is one LORD.

When one of the scribes asked Jesus, "Which is the first commandment of all?" Jesus answered him, "The first of all the commandments is, Hear, O Israel; The Lord our God is one Lord" (Mark 12:28, 29). But the Shema, the declaration of the faith of Judaism that Jesus quoted, poses a problem for Mormons. Whereas the English "God" translates the Hebrew Elohim, "LORD" represents the Hebrew tetragrammaton YHWH, the name Yahweh or Jehovah. A more literal rendering would be, "Hear, O Israel: Jehovah our Elohim is one Jehovah." This is no problem for Jews or Christians, who understand Elohim and Jehovah to be names applying to the one true God.

But Mormons have been taught that Jehovah is the premortal name of Jesus Christ, and that Elohim is the name of a different individual, namely his father. Their leaders speak of "Jehovah, who is Jesus Christ the Son of Elohim," and they say that "Among the spirit children of Elohim the firstborn was and is Jehovah or Jesus Christ to whom all others are juniors."[4] James E. Talmage, one of the Twelve Apostles of the church, declares, "Therefore we know that both the Father and the Son are in form and stature perfect men; each of them possesses a tangible body, infinitely pure and perfect and attended by transcendent glory, nevertheless a body of flesh and bones."[5]

Mormons have a problem in that the inspired declaration "the LORD our God is one LORD" is contradicted by the LDS teaching that Elohim is a perfect man with a tangible body and Jehovah is a different perfect man with his own tangible body.

See also the discussions of Genesis 1:26, 27; Exodus 6:3.

Nehemiah

Nehemiah 9:6

Thou, even thou, art LORD alone; thou hast made heaven, the heaven of heavens, with all their host, the earth, and all things that are therein, the seas, and all that is therein, and thou preservest them all; and the host of heaven worshippeth thee.

This verse is especially useful in refuting Mormon teachings about God. For example, the LDS Church teaches that all men, including Jesus Christ, were "begotten and born of heavenly parents, and reared to maturity in the eternal mansions of the Father, prior to coming upon the earth in a temporal [physical] body."[6] Moreover, Mormonism teaches that God the Father "is a glorified and perfected man, a personage of flesh and bones,"[7] that "God the Father of Jesus Christ had a Father," and that "you may suppose that He had a Father also."[8] Yet Nehemiah 9:6, quoted above, shows that the LORD made the heaven and the heaven of the heavens, with all their host—everything, the whole universe and everything and everyone in it. So how could the Creator have been reared by parents, who in turn had been reared by grandparents?

Further denying the Mormon concept of deity is Psalm 90:2, which says, "Before the mountains were brought forth, or ever thou hadst formed the earth and the world, even from everlasting to everlasting, thou art God." The Creator's being "from everlasting to everlasting" allows for no time period when he did not exist, thus no time before him when his parents could have been reared by their parents, as the LDS Church claims. Also see Psalms 93:2; 103:17; 147:4, 5.

In fact, the LORD (Jehovah) answers the question of whether parent Gods and grandparent Gods came before him:

Ye are my witnesses, saith the LORD . . . before me there was no God formed, neither shall there be after me (Isa. 43:10).
Thus saith the LORD the King of Israel, and his redeemer the LORD of hosts; I am the first, and I am the last; and beside me there is no God (Isa. 44:6).

Is there a God beside me? yea, there is no God; I know not any (Isa. 44:8).

Also see Isa. 44:24; 45:5, 6, 21; 46:9.

If we believe that God knows everything and that he would not lie to us, we must conclude that God the Creator who made everything did not have parents or grandparents preceding him, and that there are no other Gods at all; there is only the one true God. See also the discussions of Genesis 2:7; Exodus 6:3; Deuteronomy 6:4; and Daniel 7:9, 13, 22.

Psalms

Psalm 2:7

I will declare the decree: the LORD hath said unto me, Thou art my Son: this day have I begotten thee.

Some Mormons may misunderstand the word *begotten* here to refer to procreation. And so they may see Psalm 2:7 as confirming their belief that Jesus Christ was born as a spirit, the offspring of heavenly parents, and was born later as a human, the result of a physical act of procreation between God the Father and Mary. However, the inspired application of Psalm 2:7 shows that it does not support either of these claimed acts of procreation. Rather, it speaks of Christ's resurrection, as applied in Acts 13:33, 34: "He hath raised up Jesus again; as it is also written in the second psalm, Thou art my Son, this day have I begotten thee. And as concerning that he raised him up from the dead." These verses show that Psalm 2:7 refers to Christ's resurrection, not to any alleged act of procreation. Hebrews 1:5 and 5:5 also apply this verse to the resurrection.

It should also be noted that Mormons may find this verse confusing because they have been taught that "the LORD" (*YHWH*, *Yahweh*, *Jehovah*) is Jesus Christ, not God the Father. See the discussions of Exodus 6:3; Deuteronomy 6:4; and Nehemiah 9:6. See also the discussions of Matthew 1:18, 20 and Luke 1:34, 35 regarding Christ's birth.

Psalm 82:1, 6

God standeth in the congregation of the mighty; he judgeth among the gods. . . . I have said, Ye are gods; and all of you are children of the most High.

Unprepared Christians may easily be thrown off balance when shown Psalm 82. Although not a passage that Mormons normally turn to of their own initiative, at least not in the early stages of discussions, if a Christian challenges them on the issue of polytheism, they may respond by turning to Psalm 82 and saying, "Look! There it is in your own Bible. The Bible teaches what we believe." But does it really?

The psalm certainly does speak of "gods" who are "children of the most High," but this language must be understood in the light of other Bible passages which teach that "there is one God" (1 Tim. 2:5). In Isaiah chapter 44 God says, "I am the first, and I am the last; and beside me there is no God. . . . Is there a God beside me? yea, there is no God; I know not any" (vv. 6 and 8).

Since God has thus made it clear that there are no other gods, why is the plural term *gods* used in Psalm 82? Paul says there are many "that are called gods, whether in heaven or in earth" (1 Cor. 8:5). Idols are called gods by those who worship them, yet verse 4 says that an idol is really "nothing" because "there is none other God but one." Psalm 82 is not addressed to idols, of course, but those to whom the words are addressed are likewise called gods. Who are they? Evidently they are human judges who "judge unjustly" (v. 2) and who fail to "do justice to the afflicted and needy." (v. 3) Because of their failure to judge justly, God himself will arise to judge them and all the earth (vv. 1 and 8).

Human judges might be called gods because they exercise authority over men, or because they stand in God's place when passing judgment. If judging rightly, proclaiming and enforcing God's laws, they would be acting as his spokesmen or representatives. (Compare Exodus 4:16, where the Lord said Moses would be "instead of God" to his brother Aaron.)

In any case, those addressed as gods in Psalm 82 were themselves to be judged, to fall, and to die—certainly not the fate of real "gods" (v. 7). In spite of appearances to the contrary, Psalm 82 does not support Mormonism's polytheistic theology.

See also the discussions of John 10:34 and 1 Corinthians 8:5, and chapter 2, "What the Mormon Church Teaches."

Psalm 110:4

The LORD hath sworn, and will not repent, Thou art a priest for ever after the order of Melchizedek.

Mormonism claims to possess within its church organization the restored Melchizedek Priesthood, identifying the Latter-day Saints as the only true worshipers on earth today. But the context of Psalm 110:4 shows that the prophecy points forward to the Messiah, and the New Testament in Hebrews chapters 5 through 8 applies it to Christ alone, who "needs no successor" in the priesthood (Heb. 7:24 *Phillips*).

See also the discussions of Genesis 14:18 and Acts 3:20, 21.

Isaiah

Isaiah 29:4, 11

And thou shalt be brought down, and shalt speak out of the ground, and thy speech shall be low out of the dust, and thy voice shall be, as of one that hath a familiar spirit, out of the ground, and thy speech shall whisper out of the dust. . . . And the vision of all is become unto you as the words of a book that is sealed.

Isaiah's prophecy is concerning Jerusalem, "the city where David dwelt" (v. 1). Yet, because portions of the prophecy are reproduced nearly word for word in the Book of Mormon, the LDS Church applies Isaiah's prophecy to the Nephite people who, they claim, inhabited North America centuries ago. (Compare Isa. 29:1–4 with 2 Nephi 26:15–17.) Isaiah's telling the Jews that prophetic vision had been sealed up to them like a sealed book is taken out of context and explained as a reference to the Book of Mormon allegedly having been hidden away in the ground.

Yet the most amazing aspect of Mormon misapplication of Isaiah's prophecy is the reference to "a familiar spirit" in Isaiah 29:4. Typically, Mormon missionaries will encourage a Bible-reading Christian to read the Book of Mormon and to notice that it has "a familiar spirit," meaning that the Christian will find things that he is already familiar with or accustomed to. Mormon author LeGrand Richards puts it this way in his book *A Marvelous Work And A Wonder:* "Now, obviously, the only way a dead people could speak 'out of the ground' or 'low out of the dust' would be by the written word, and this the people did through the Book of Mormon. Truly it has a familiar spirit, for it contains the words of the prophets of the God of Israel" (1979 edition, pp. 67–68).

Richards, who was a member of the LDS Council of the Twelve Apostles, boasts that the Book of Mormon "has a familiar spirit" and that it was prophesied by Isaiah. This is amazing, because whenever the Bible speaks of "a familiar spirit" it refers to a spirit person who is familiar or intimate with humans, communicating with them through a witch or a spirit medium. And in every case the one who has the familiar spirit is condemned by God.

For example, Deuteronomy 18:9–12 includes "a consulter with familiar spirits" among the practicers of spiritism to be excluded from Israel:

> When thou art come into the land which the LORD thy God giveth thee, thou shalt not learn to do after the abominations of those nations. There shall not be found among you any one that maketh his son or his daughter to pass through the fire, or that useth divination, or an observer of times, or an enchanter, or a witch, or a charmer, or a consulter with familiar spirits, or a wizard, or a necromancer. For all that do these things are an abomination unto the LORD.

Consulting someone who had a familiar spirit was grounds for the divine judgment of death in the case of King Saul (1 Chron. 10:13):

> So Saul died for his transgression which he committed against the LORD, even against the word of the LORD, which he kept not, and also for asking counsel of one that had a familiar spirit, to enquire of it.

Similarly, dealing with a familiar spirit was classified as evil in the case of King Manasseh (2 Chron. 33:6):

> And he caused his children to pass through the fire in the valley of the son of Hinnom: also he observed times, and used enchantments, and used witchcraft, and dealt with a familiar spirit, and with wizards: he wrought much evil in the sight of the LORD, to provoke him to anger.

Joseph Smith, Jr., the founder of Mormonism who claimed to have miraculously translated the Book of Mormon from gold plates, had previously been tried in a New York court as a "glass-looker" who practiced "money digging" by means of divination. If his Book of Mormon truly does have "a familiar spirit" in the sense in which Isaiah and other Bible writers used the term, the verses just quoted give us good reason *not* to consult it as a sacred book.

See also the discussion of the Book of Mormon in chapter 3, "Mormon Scripture."

Jeremiah

Jeremiah 1:5

Before I formed thee in the belly I knew thee; and before thou camest forth out of the womb I sanctified thee, and I ordained thee a prophet unto the nations.

The Mormon apologist will say God knew Jeremiah before he was born and also before he was "formed in the belly," before he was even conceived in the womb. This is proof that "we all lived in the spirit before we were born in the flesh," according to the Mormon text *A Marvelous Work And A Wonder* (page 39). "Jeremiah could not have been so called and ordained before he was born if he did not exist," it adds.

Does this prove that we all lived in the spirit before we were born in the flesh? No, because the Bible states clearly that the exact opposite is true: "That was not first which is spiritual, but that which is natural; and afterward that which is spiritual" (1 Cor. 15:46). Man's spirit does not pre-exist independently of the body; rather, the Bible says that God "formeth the spirit of man within him" (Zech. 12:1). Thus, when God asked Job, "Where wast thou when I laid the foundations of the earth? declare, if thou hast understanding," Job was left speechless, because he had not yet come into existence at the time God was speaking about (Job 38:4; 40:3–5).

Still, Mormons will insist that God's "knowing" Jeremiah before he formed him in the belly logically implies that Jeremiah existed somewhere before conception. And we can agree that such a conclusion is indeed logical from a human perspective, but we should remind them that it was God who knew Jeremiah before his birth and conception, and "The things which are impossible with men are possible with God" (Luke 18:27). It is "God who quickeneth the dead, and calleth those things which be not as though they were" (Rom. 4:17). He was able to call and ordain Jeremiah even when Jeremiah did *not* yet exist. The Creator is the one "Declaring the end from the beginning, and from ancient times the things that are not yet done" (Isa. 46:10).

With his divine ability to look into the future, it is no problem
for God to know someone who does not yet exist.

See also the discussions of John 17:5 and Acts 17:28, 29.

Ezekiel

Ezekiel 37:16, 17

Moreover, thou son of man, take thee one stick, and write upon
it, For Judah, and for the children of Israel his companions: then
take another stick, and write upon it, For Joseph, the stick of
Ephraim, and for all the house of Israel his companions: And join
them one to another into one stick; and they shall become one in
thine hand.

Mormons use these verses as a biblical justification for the
Book of Mormon. Since a stick may have been used in ancient
times to support a scroll of parchment, they say that the stick of
Judah is the Bible, the written record of the Jews. What then is
the stick of Joseph? It must be another sacred book, the Book of
Mormon, the record of Joseph's descendants who migrated to the
Americas.

However, in attempting to stretch God's words as recorded by
Ezekiel into an endorsement for the Book of Mormon, they ignore
the context. In the next few verses, Ezekiel records God's own
explanation of what is really meant by the two sticks:

And when the children of thy people shall speak unto thee, saying, Wilt thou not shew us what thou meanest by these? . . . And
say unto them, Thus saith the Lord GOD; Behold, I will take the
children of Israel from among the heathen, whither they be gone,
and will gather them on every side, and bring them into their own
land: And I will make them one nation in the land upon the
mountains of Israel; and one king shall be king to them all: and
they shall be no more two nations, neither shall they be divided
into two kingdoms any more at all (Ezek. 37:18, 21, 22).

The meaning of the two sticks is plainly explained here in the
same chapter of Ezekiel, and it has nothing to do with the Book
of Mormon. When the twelve tribes of Israel escaped from

bondage in Egypt and settled the promised land, each had its own tribal territory. After the death of King Solomon the nation split into two kingdoms along tribal lines. The southern kingdom consisted of the territories of Judah and Benjamin, with the majority of territory and power belonging to Judah. The remaining tribal territories made up the northern kingdom, with the offspring of Joseph's sons Ephraim and Manasseh holding the lion's share of the land. Therefore, the stick of Judah represented the tribes of the southern kingdom, and the stick of Joseph represented the tribes of the northern kingdom. God said that he had Ezekiel join the two sticks into one to visually demonstrate his promise that "I will make them one nation . . . and they shall be no more two nations, neither shall they be divided into two kingdoms any more at all" (Ezek. 37:22).

Daniel

Daniel 7:9, 13, 22

I beheld till the thrones were cast down, and the Ancient of days did sit, whose garment was white as snow, and the hair of his head like the pure wool: his throne was like the fiery flame, and his wheels as burning fire. . . . I saw in the night visions, and, behold, one like the Son of man came with the clouds of heaven, and came to the Ancient of days, and they brought him near before him. . . . Until the Ancient of days came, and judgment was given to the saints of the most High; and the time came that the saints possessed the kingdom.

Orthodox Christians believe that the Ancient of days in Daniel 7 is God the Father, the first person of the Trinity. Jewish people believe that he is the one true God, Jehovah (Yahweh). Likewise, Christians believe that the Son of man refers to Jesus, and that Daniel is a prophetic book that refers to the end times and judgment.

Mormons, on the other hand, have extra-biblical revelation that says the Ancient of days is Adam, the first man, and Michael the Archangel. Doctrine and Covenants 27:11 (given by Joseph Smith in August 1830) says, "And also with Michael, or Adam, the father of all, the prince of all, the ancient of days." Section

116 says, "Adam shall come to visit his people, or the Ancient of Days shall sit, as spoken of by Daniel the prophet." D & C 138:38 refers to "Father Adam, the Ancient of Days and father of all."

On April 9, 1852, Brigham Young shocked Mormons and the world with his oft-quoted (or misquoted) Adam-God discourse, published in *Journal of Discourses*, vol. 1:50–51 and in *Millennial Star*, vol. 15, November 26, 1853. The heading in *Millennial Star* and *Journal of Discourses* 1:46 says, "ADAM, Our Father and Our GOD." Page 50 announces this new teaching:

> Now hear it, O inhabitants of the earth, Jew and Gentile, Saint and Sinner! When our father Adam came into the garden of Eden, he came into it with a *celestial body*, and brought Eve, *one of his wives*, with him. He helped to make and organize this world. He is MICHAEL, *the Archangel*, the ANCIENT OF DAYS! about whom holy men have written and spoken—HE *is our* FATHER *and our* GOD, *and the only God with whom* WE *have to do.* . . . When the Virgin Mary conceived the child Jesus, the Father had begotten him in his own likeness. He was *not* begotten by the Holy Ghost. And who is the Father? He is the first of the human family. [emphasis in original]

Parts of this discourse on page 51 not usually quoted are:

> It is true that this earth was organized by three distinct characters, namely, Eloheim, Yahovah, and Michael, these three forming a quorum . . . perfectly represented in the Deity, as Father, Son, and Holy Ghost. . . . Now let all who may hear these doctrines, pause before they make light of them, or treat them with indifference, for they will prove their salvation or damnation.

Note the words "will prove their salvation or damnation." This Adam God teaching was considered very important by Brigham Young. He taught that Adam was not only our God, but also the father of our spirits, that Jesus was his firstborn spirit and the *only begotten* of Adam in the flesh. He consistently taught this doctrine as recorded in his sermons. It was believed by many of his followers and recorded in their diaries and journals, but was vigorously disputed by others. On June 18, 1873, *The Deseret News* published one of his clearest talks on this subject (p. 308, col. 4):

> How much unbelief exists in the minds of the Latter-day Saints in regard to one particular doctrine which I revealed to them and which God revealed to me—namely that Adam is our Father and our God. . . . Our Father Adam helped to make this earth, it was created expressly for him. . . . He brought one of his wives with him, and she was called Eve.

In column 5 of this article Brigham Young continues:

> "Why was Adam called Adam?" He was the first man on the earth, and its framer and maker. He with the help of his brethren, brought it into existence. Then he said, "I want my children who are in the spirit world to come and live here. I once dwelt upon an earth something like this, in a mortal state. I was faithful. I received my crown and exaltation. I have the privilege of extending my work, and to its increase there will be no end. I want my children that were born to me in the spirit world to come here and take tabernacles of flesh, that their spirits may have a house, a tabernacle or a dwelling place as mine has and, where is the mystery?"

This discourse is perfectly consistent with the Mormon doctrine that only resurrected beings can procreate "spirit offspring"[9] and that Adam had no blood when he came to earth, not until after he ate of the fruit.[10]

Lest there be any doubt about who Brigham Young thought the Ancient of days was, look at *Journal of Discourses* 11:327 (Feb. 10, 1867):

> They will come up tribe, by tribe, and the Ancient of Days, He who led Abraham, and talked to Noah, Enoch, Isaac, and Jacob, that very Being will come and judge the twelve tribes of Israel.

The Adam-God doctrine is *not* now taught by the Mormon Church. In fact, the twelfth Mormon President and Prophet Spencer W. Kimball denounced it strongly as false doctrine

(*Church News*, October 9, 1976). When referred to at all today it is called the *Adam-God theory*.

The primary argument of Mormons who do not accept the Adam-God theory or doctrine is that it is not scriptural; and those who do accept the fact that Brigham Young actually taught it reject it because it was not presented to the membership for a "common consent" vote. However, a comparison of Daniel 7:9, 13, 14, 22 with the following Mormon canonized scripture verses show that the doctrine was already in Mormon scripture and therefore a membership vote was not required:

> And also with Michael, or Adam, the father of all, the prince of all, the ancient of days (Doctrine and Covenants 27:11).
> Spring Hill is named by the Lord Adam-ondi-Ahman, because, said he, it is the place where Adam shall come to visit his people, or the Ancient of Days shall sit, as spoken of by Daniel the prophet (Doctrine and Covenants 116:1).

Moreover, this verse, dated 1918, but not in D & C until 1982, further confirms the teaching:

> Among the great and mighty ones who were assembled in this vast congregation of the righteous were Father Adam, the Ancient of Days and father of all (Doctrine and Covenants 138:38).

The 1979 edition of the Mormon Church's King James Bible under Daniel 7:9–14 lists these as cross references: Rev. 5:11; 11:18; 19:20; 20:10; 20:12; Malachi 3:16; TG [*Topical Guide*] Judgment, The Last; TG Jesus Christ, Second Coming of; Jesus Christ, Son of Man; TG Jesus Christ, Millennial Reign; and so on. So the person sitting on the throne in Daniel is the person sitting on the throne in Revelation. And in Revelation it is "our God which sitteth upon the throne" (Rev. 1:4; 3:21; 7:10, 15; 14:5; 22:1).

This is a very good topic for Christians to discuss with Mormons or with "investigators"—persons studying with missionaries to learn Mormonism. (Be aware, though, that the LDS Church claims this is a false doctrine made up by enemies of the church.) If you begin with the verses in Daniel chapter 7 and ask *who* is sitting on the throne, more than likely a Mormon will answer "God." Then turn to the parallel passages in Revelation cited above. When he or she is fully convinced that this is God on the throne, then look up together the Mormon scriptures in Doctrine and Covenants that say that the Ancient of days is Adam. If possible, show photocopies[11] of the pertinent Brigham Young discourses in context; if you simply quote a portion, you will be accused of taking it out of context. The Mormon has to see it for himself.

See also the discussion of Genesis 2:7.

Amos

Amos 3:7

Surely the Lord GOD will do nothing, but he revealeth his secret unto his servants the prophets.

If leaders of the LDS Church are prophets, as claimed, then the above words must apply to them. But history has shown the opposite to be the case.

Take, for example, the murder of Joseph Smith. Shortly before he was killed he wrote in *The History of the Church*:

> This generation is as corrupt as the generation of the Jews that crucified Christ; and if He were here to-day, and should preach the same doctrine He did then, they would put Him to death. I defy all the world to destroy the work of God; and I prophesy they will never have power to kill me till my work is accomplished, and I am ready to die (October 15, 1843, vol. 6, p. 58).

On June 27, 1844, less than nine months later, Joseph Smith was shot to death at Carthage, Illinois, by an armed mob. Evidently not "ready to die," he fired shots in his own defense and attempted to escape his attackers by leaping from a window. Unlike Jesus Christ, who correctly prophesied his own death, Joseph Smith predicted that he would *not* be killed—hardly what would be expected of a prophet, in view of the inspired statement of Amos 3:7.

Smith's successor as prophet of the LDS Church, Brigham Young, taught as follows concerning the practice of plural marriage:

> Do you think that we shall ever be admitted as a State into the Union without denying the principle of polygamy? If we are not admitted until then, we shall never be admitted (August 19, 1866, *Journal of Discourses*, vol. 11, p. 269).

Yet, history records that the LDS Church issued an official declaration in 1890 ending polygamy, prior to Utah's admission to the Union. This "prophet," too, was misinformed about what the Lord would do. Since the problem could not be with the Lord or his inspired word, the failure of Amos 3:7 to apply to them can only be because Joseph Smith and Brigham Young were not truly prophets of God.

5

Verse-by-Verse Answers for Mormons: New Testament

Matthew

Matthew 1:18, 20

Now the birth of Jesus Christ was on this wise: When as his mother Mary was espoused to Joseph, before they came together, she was found with child of the Holy Ghost. . . . That which is conceived in her is of the Holy Ghost.

These are verses[1] that Christians may wish to turn to in discussions with Mormons. Why? Because Mormon leader Brigham Young flatly denied their truthfulness. In a talk recorded at a General Conference of the LDS Church, Brigham Young said:

> When the virgin Mary conceived the child Jesus, the Father had begotten him in his own likeness. He was *not* begotten by the Holy Ghost. And who is the Father? He is the first of the human family [Adam]. . . .
> Jesus, our elder brother, was begotten in the flesh by the same character that was in the garden of Eden, and who is our Father in Heaven. Now, let all who may hear these doctrines pause before they make light of them, or treat them with indifference, for they will prove their salvation or damnation.

. . . Now remember from this time forth, and for ever, that Jesus
Christ was not begotten by the Holy Ghost (Brigham Young,
Journal of Discourses, vol. 1, pp. 50, 51, April 9, 1852; also, *The
Latter-Day Saints' MILLENNIAL STAR*, vol. XV, No. 48,
Saturday, November 26, 1853, pp. 769, 770).

This teaching given at a General Conference of the Mormon
Church by Brigham Young flatly contradicts the Bible's statement
that Mary was "with child of the Holy Ghost." Why? Because
Mormons have been taught that "the Holy Ghost is a male personage. . . . the Holy Ghost is a personage of spirit in the form of a
man."[2] To Mormons, God the Father and the Holy Ghost are two
different Gods, and only one of them could be the father of Jesus.
Since it was God the Father, then it was not the Holy Ghost who
was Jesus' male parent. Although Mormons claim to believe in
the Bible, they allow their leaders and scriptures to overrule and
contradict the Bible, giving them higher authority than the book
Christians accept as God's Word.

See also the discussion of Luke 1:34, 35.

Matthew 3:16, 17

And Jesus, when he was baptized, went up straightway out of the
water: and, lo, the heavens were opened unto him, and he saw the
Spirit of God descending like a dove, and lighting upon him: And lo
a voice from heaven, saying, This is my beloved Son, in whom I am
well pleased.

On one occasion a Mormon read these verses to a Christian
and, thinking that the Christian believed Jesus Christ and God
the Father to be the same person, he asked somewhat sarcasti-
cally, "When the God Jesus came out of the water was he acting
as a ventriloquist and throwing his voice so that it would sound
like it was coming from heaven?"

Other Mormon missionaries may make the same point by reading these verses and then arguing in this manner: "Here God the
Father, Jesus Christ, and the Holy Spirit are shown to be separate
and distinct persons located in different places and each one
doing something different: the Father speaking from heaven, Jesus

coming up out of the water of baptism, and the Holy Spirit float-
ing down through the air like a bird. This disproves the belief that
the three are one person without body or form, as taught in the
various churches."

If the unsuspecting householder finds his faith shaken by such
arguments, it is for two reasons: (1) he started out with a popular
misconception in his own mind rather than with sound Christian
theology, and (2) the Mormon missionaries played upon this by
misrepresenting Christian belief. True, there may be *some* pseudo-
Christian sects that present God as a vague, nebulous person, but
that is not what is taught in sound, Bible-believing churches.
Christians who are readers of Holy Scripture know that the
Father is God, the Son is God, and the Holy Spirit is God, and
yet there is only one true God; so they conclude, in agreement
with traditional church teaching, that God is triune, that the
three distinct persons making up the Divinity are together the
one true God.

While a reading of Matthew 3:16 and 17 might unsettle someone who thinks the Christian churches present God as a single
incorporeal person, and while some Mormon missionaries might
successfully attack this concept in an attempt to turn their potential converts to Mormonism, such an off-target argument will have
no effect on Christians who *know* the God they worship.

See also the discussion of Genesis 1:26, 27.

Matthew 5:48

Be ye therefore perfect, even as your Father which is in heaven is
perfect.

Some Mormons reason as follows: Would God give us a commandment we could not keep? The obvious answer is no (see
1 Cor. 10:13). They then turn to Matthew 5:48 and say that it
means we should have all the attributes of God; therefore, we can
become Gods. In doing this, however, they make two major mistakes. They ignore what *perfect* really means in the biblical context, and they assume it leads to Godhood.

The Bible is very clear that we are all sinners (Rom. 3:10, 23;
1 John 1:8–10; Isa. 64:6). We know from Genesis 6:9 that Noah

was just and perfect, and from Job 1:1 that Job was perfect. These men were sinners as we know from the above verses, so *perfect* clearly does not mean "sinless," as the Mormons would have us believe. The Greek word *teleioi* is translated as "perfect" in Matthew 5:48 and also means "complete," "mature," "ended." But at our best we will only be "perfect" *people*. There is nothing in the Bible about "perfect" humans progressing to Godhood. We can be complete, mature, perfect people as God the Father is complete, mature, perfect, but we will always be human.

Matthew 15:24

But he answered and said, I am not sent but unto the lost sheep of the house of Israel.

A footnote to this verse in the LDS Salt Lake City Bible ties in the "lost sheep of the house of Israel" with the "scattering" of Israel, representatives of the tribe of Joseph allegedly having migrated to the Americas. Book of Mormon verses in the Topical Guide section cited in this footnote tell of Jesus' alleged visits to these Israelites in the Americas.

But, is that what Jesus meant when he referred to "the lost sheep of the house of Israel"? No. Rather, he meant the Israelites to whom he was preaching in Judah and in Galilee who were in a "lost" condition in God's eyes. This is clear from the way he used the same expression earlier in Matthew's Gospel when he sent out his apostles into towns he himself was about to visit, instructing them, "Go not into the way of the Gentiles, and into any city of the Samaritans enter ye not: But go rather to the lost sheep of the house of Israel" (Matt. 10:5, 6). Obviously, he did not send them to the Americas.

See also the discussions of Genesis 37:5, 10; John 10:16; and 3 Nephi 15:17, 21, 22.

Luke

Luke 1:34, 35

Then said Mary unto the angel, How shall this be, seeing I know not a man? And the angel answered and said unto her, The Holy Ghost shall come upon thee, and the power of the Highest shall

overshadow thee: therefore also that holy thing which shall be born
of thee shall be called the Son of God.

Although obscured today by an LDS Church working hard to
improve its public image, the Mormon version of the birth of
Christ is quite different from the understanding of it Christians
derive from the Bible alone. The doctrine introduced by Brigham
Young and confirmed by other General Authorities of the church
is basically this: that God the Father—a male person with a body
of flesh and bones—visited the virgin Mary and physically
fathered Jesus Christ. *Family Home Evening Manual*, a book published by the Mormon Church for parents to use in home studies
with their children, puts it this way: "Well, now for the benefit of
the older ones, how are children begotten? I answer just as Jesus
Christ was begotten of his father" (1972 edition, p. 125).

This says that God the Father procreated Jesus through sexual
relations with Mary. This is, in fact, one of the hidden doctrines
of Mormonism. Brigham Young taught this on numerous occasions: "The birth of the Saviour was as natural as are the births of
our children: it was the result of natural action. He partook of
flesh and blood—was begotten of his Father, as we were of our
fathers" (1860, *Journal of Discourses*, vol. 8, p. 115). "When the
time came that His first born, the Saviour, should come into the
world and take a tabernacle [body], the Father came Himself and
favoured that spirit with a tabernacle instead of letting any other
man do it" (1857, *Journal of Discourses*, vol. 4, p. 218).

When defending the doctrine of polygamy Brigham Young
added, "This matter was a little changed in the case of the Savior
of the world, the Son of the living God. The man Joseph, the
husband of Mary, did not, that we know of, have more than one
wife, but Mary the wife of Joseph had another husband" (1866,
Journal of Discourses, vol. 11, p. 268).

This teaching on the birth of Christ was by no means limited
to Brigham Young, but was understood and taught by other con-
temporary LDS Church leaders: "I was naturally begotten; so was
my father, and also my Saviour Jesus Christ. According to the
Scriptures, he is the first begotten of his father in the flesh, and

there was nothing unnatural about it" (Heber C. Kimball, 1860, *Journal of Discourses*, vol. 8, p. 211).

And, lest any Mormon deny that the LDS Church teaches this today (some may be ignorant of the doctrine, and some, although aware of it, may feel that others are not ready to hear it), it can be found in *The Articles of Faith: Being a Consideration of the Principal Doctrines of The Church of Jesus Christ of Latter-day Saints*, by James E. Talmage. In Appendix 2 on page 473 this work refers to Christ's "unique status in the flesh as the offspring of a mortal mother and of an immortal, or resurrected and glorified, Father." And the teaching is confirmed in the more recent (1966) text *Mormon Doctrine*, by Bruce McConkie: "Begotten means begotten; and Son means son. Christ was begotten by an Immortal Father in the same way that mortal men are begotten by mortal fathers" (p. 547). "There is nothing figurative about his paternity; he was begotten, conceived and born in the normal and natural course of events, for he is the Son of God, and that designation means what it says" (p. 742).

In presenting this doctrine Brigham Young knew how it would be received by outsiders, particularly Christians. He said, "I could tell you much more about this; but were I to tell you the whole truth, blasphemy would be nothing to it, in the estimation of the superstitious and over-righteous of mankind" (Brigham Young, *The Latter-Day Saints MILLENNIAL STAR*, 1853, vol. 15, p. 770). On this point we agree with Brigham Young, that his doctrine is in fact blasphemy—and one does not have to be "over-righteous" to appreciate that fact.

See also the discussions of Psalm 2:7; Daniel 7:9, 13, 22; and Matthew 1:18, 20.

Luke 24:39

Behold my hands and my feet, that it is I myself: handle me, and see, for a spirit hath not flesh and bones, as ye see me have.

LDS Apostle LeGrand Richards quotes this verse to refute the idea that Jesus is "without body or form, so large that he fills the universe and so small that he dwells in each heart, as so many believe and as the churches teach" (*A Marvelous Work And A*

Wonder, 1979 edition, pp. 18–19). But is that really what the churches teach? Not the Bible-believing ones.

The bodily resurrection of Christ is one of the basic tenets of orthodox Christianity. No sound Christian church would describe him as "without body or form." Rather, "in him dwelleth all the fullness of the Godhead bodily" (Col. 2:9).

Although he has a body of flesh and bones, the resurrected Christ is able to appear and disappear at will, with walls and locked doors serving as no obstacle to him (Luke 24:31, 36; John 20:19, 26). Although "we shall be like him" in the resurrection, "it doth not yet appear what we shall be" (1 John 3:2). God has not furnished us, in advance, much information about the resurrection body, except that it is "changed" from and superior to what we have now (1 Cor. 15:35–53).

Moreover, when Christians believe "That Christ may dwell in your hearts by faith" (Eph. 3:17), this does not require that he become so small that his body can fit inside a human heart. Although the Bible speaks of "this mystery . . . which is Christ in you" (Col. 1:27), it also explains that "God hath sent forth the Spirit of his Son into your hearts, crying, Abba, Father" (Gal. 4:6). He does not enter bodily into our hearts.

While the Mormon argument presented above in connection with Luke 24:39 might shake someone with a nebulous concept of Christ, it should not prove troubling to Bible-believing Christians.

John

John 1:18

No man hath seen God at any time; the only begotten Son, which is in the bosom of the Father, he hath declared him.

Since Joseph Smith claimed to have seen God the Father, this verse proved to be a problem for him. However, rather than back off from his claim of having seen God, he sought to change Scripture. Thus Mormons are able to turn to their Doctrine and Covenants and read, "For no man has seen God at any time in the flesh, except quickened by the Spirit of God"—from a revela-

72

Mormons Answered Verse by Verse

tion allegedly received by Joseph Smith in November, 1831 (Doctrine and Covenants 67:11).

Not satisfied simply to have added this 'exception' by means of a personal revelation, Smith went on to retranslate the text of John's Gospel itself. Thus his "translation" of the Bible presents John 1:19[3] as saying, "And no man hath seen God at any time, except he hath borne record of the Son; for except it is through him no man can be saved."

On what basis did Smith change the Bible text to conform to his thinking? Did he render some Greek words differently to produce this new wording? No, because the Greek words in the manuscripts Bible translators have been using for years could not possibly be rendered that way. Did Smith discover other ancient manuscripts with different wording? No, he did not claim any such discovery. On what basis, then, did he produce such a radically different "translation"? Again, the claim was that he was personally "inspired" to do so—even though his rendering has no basis in any existing ancient manuscript and in fact contradicts the hundreds of Greek manuscripts preserved from ancient times.

It should also be pointed out to Mormons that Joseph Smith's claim to have seen God the Father and Jesus Christ in his "First Vision" also contradicts Mormon scripture. Doctrine and Covenants 84:21, 22 says that "without the ordinances . . . and the authority" of the Melchizedek Priesthood, "without this no man can see the face of God, even the Father, and live." Yet Smith claimed to see God the Father in his "First Vision" several years *before* he allegedly received the Melchizedek Priesthood.

See also the discussions of Genesis 32:30, Exodus 24:10, 11; 33:11; Deuteronomy 4:2; 1 John 4:12; and chapter 3, "Mormon Scripture."

John 6:46

Not that any man hath seen the Father, save he which is of God, he hath seen the Father.

Mormons will explain this verse by turning to their Doctrine and Covenants 67:11 and reading, "For no man has seen God at any time in the flesh, except quickened by the Spirit of God."

Although these words formed part of a "revelation" Joseph Smith claimed to have received at Hiram, Ohio, November 1831, "This is apparently what John had in mind" when writing John 6:46, according to Mormon Apostle LeGrand Richards (*A Marvelous Work And A Wonder*, 1979 edition, p. 21).

However, persons not already indoctrinated with LDS teachings are unlikely to believe that John had in mind a doctrine to be "revealed" some eighteen centuries later by Joseph Smith. Rather, what John had in mind is evident from the context. In fact, it was not John but Jesus Christ who was speaking, and he was speaking about himself and his having come down from heaven where he had, of course, seen the Father:

> The Jews then murmured at him, because he said, I am the bread which came down from heaven. And they said, Is not this Jesus, the son of Joseph, whose father and mother we know? how is it then that he saith, I came down from heaven? . . . Every man therefore that hath heard, and hath learned of the Father, cometh unto me. Not that any man hath seen the Father, save he which is of God, he hath seen the Father. Verily, verily, I say unto you, He that believeth on me hath everlasting life . . . I am the living bread which came down from heaven. . . . The living Father hath sent me. . . . What and if ye shall see the Son of man ascend up where he was before? (John 6:41, 42, 45–47, 51, 57, 62).

The context makes it obvious what Jesus had in mind when he said, "Not that any man hath seen the Father, save he which is of God, he hath seen the Father." He had in mind that *he* had come down from heaven, that *he* had been sent by the Father, and that *he* was the only man who had ever seen the Father. The only way that Mormons are able to come up with a different understanding is to appeal to writings outside the Bible and contradictory to it.

See also the discussions of John 1:18 and 1 John 4:12.

John 10:16

And other sheep I have, which are not of this fold: them also I must bring, and they shall hear my voice; and there shall be one fold, and one shepherd.

Mormons see in this verse a reference to the alleged visit of Christ to the inhabitants of the Western Hemisphere, as related in the Book of Mormon. Who else could these "other sheep" be, they ask, than Israelites living in the New World?

Christian commentators apply this expression to Gentiles, people not of the house of Israel. But Mormons answer that this could not be, since Jesus was sent only "unto the lost sheep of the house of Israel" (Matt. 15:24). They reason that Jesus preached only to the descendants of Israel's son Judah during his ministry in Palestine, and that "a remnant of the house of Joseph" heard his voice when he visited them in the Western Hemisphere.[4]

In discussions with Christians who, of course, do not believe in the Book of Mormon, LDS missionaries may use the above line of reasoning to support their interpretation of John 10:16. But the real reason they believe this interpretation is that it is spelled out for them in the Book of Mormon. The words of Jesus at John 10:16 are repeated (following the King James Bible word for word) in the Book of Mormon at 3 Nephi 15:17 and again at 3 Nephi 15:21 and are discussed in detail throughout the fifteenth and sixteenth chapters of 3 Nephi. The speaker is alleged to be Jesus himself during a visit in the year A.D. 34 to the Nephite people of America, whom he identifies as the "other sheep" referred to in his earlier talk at Jerusalem. See the discussion of 3 Nephi 15:17, 21, 22 for more on this portion of Mormon scripture.

When Jesus started his ministry it was aimed at the "lost sheep of the house of Israel" (Matt. 15:22–28). He traveled through Judea, Galilee, and Samaria, and the Jews who eventually put faith in him were not limited to descendants of Judah but also included members of the Israelite tribes of Benjamin (Rom. 11:1) and Asher (Luke 2:36), indeed individuals from "all the house of Israel" (Acts 2:36).

In addition, God had said through the Hebrew prophets that "I will provoke you [Israel] to jealousy by them that are no people, and by a foolish nation I will anger you. . . . I was found of them that sought me not; I was made manifest unto them that asked not after me" (Rom. 10:19, 29). This description would not fit the Nephite or Lamanite peoples claimed by the Mormons to have received a visit from Christ in the New World. But it would fit the Gentiles. And the Scriptures show clearly that the sheep flocking to Christ as their shepherd would eventually include Gentiles:

> Behold my servant, whom I have chosen; my beloved, in whom my soul is well pleased: I will put my spirit upon him, and he shall shew judgment to the Gentiles. . . . And in his name shall the Gentiles trust (Matt. 12:18, 21).
>
> But the Lord said unto him, Go thy way: for he is a chosen vessel unto me, to bear my name before the Gentiles (Acts 9:15).
>
> Be it known therefore unto you, that the salvation of God is sent unto the Gentiles, and that they will hear it (Acts 28:28).

See also the discussion of Matthew 15:24.

John 10:34

Jesus answered them, Is it not written in your law, I said, Ye are gods?

Jesus was quoting here from Psalm 82:6. Was he thus express-ing support for the LDS doctrine of the plurality of Gods? Let's look at the context. Certain Jews picked up stones to throw at Jesus, accusing him of blasphemy "because that thou, being a man, makest thyself God" (John 10:33). Jesus responded with the words quoted above and then continued: "If he called them gods, unto whom the word of God came, and the scripture cannot be broken; Say ye of him, whom the Father hath sanctified, and sent into the world, Thou blasphemest; because I said, I am the Son of God?" (vv. 35, 36).

Rather than testifying to the plurality of Gods, Jesus was here making a contrast. He was contrasting himself with those who were called gods in Psalm 82. The Jews listening were familiar with the psalm and knew that the word of God was spoken *against* those individuals who were thus referred to. The point Jesus made, in effect, was "If individuals like *that* can be called 'gods,' how can you object to my saying I am God's Son?" He was not teaching polytheistic theology.

See the discussions of Psalm 82:1, 6 and 1 Corinthians 8:5; also chapter 2, "What the Mormon Church Teaches."

John 17:5

And now, O Father, glorify thou me with thine own self with the glory which I had with thee before the world was.

In his book *A Marvelous Work And A Wonder* Mormon author LeGrand Richards uses this verse to prove that "we all lived in the spirit before we were born in the flesh" (1979 edition, p. 39). The LDS Church teaches that we each had a prior existence before being born here on earth, that we lived as spirits with God before getting our human bodies. But does what Jesus said here really prove this about all of us? Well, did *everything* that happened to Jesus Christ also happen to you? Were you born in Bethlehem? of a virgin? without a human father? to die on the cross and rise three days later? No, of course not! So, if the other circumstances of Jesus' unique life do not reflect our circumstances, there is no basis to assume that his prior existence finds a parallel in us.

In fact, Jesus declared that "no man hath ascended up to heaven, but he that came down from heaven, even the Son of man which is in heaven" (John 3:13). No other man had a prior existence before birth—only Jesus Christ.

See also the discussions of Jeremiah 1:5, and Acts 17:28, 29, verses used by Mormons to "prove" that ordinary people lived as spirits before being born.

Acts

Acts 3:20, 21

And he shall send Jesus Christ, which before was preached unto you: Whom the heaven must receive until the times of restitution of all things, which God hath spoken by the mouth of all his holy prophets since the world began.

Christians understand these verses as referring to the millennial reign of Christ. But when discussing their claims to priesthood Mormon missionaries may refer an inquirer to the chapter on "Restoration of Priesthood Authority" in LeGrand Richard's book *A Marvelous Work And A Wonder*, which, on page 82 (1979 edition), applies the above scripture thus:

> Therefore, in order that there might be a "restitution of all things, which God hath spoken by the mouth of all his holy prophets since the world began" (see Acts 3:21), it was necessary that these two priesthoods be restored again to men upon this earth.

The Aaronic Priesthood was restored on May 15, 1829, so the story goes, when John the Baptist appeared to Joseph Smith and Oliver Cowdery and conferred it upon them. The Melchizedek Priesthood was allegedly restored when the apostles Peter, James, and John made a similar visitation at an undisclosed date. Then Joseph Smith passed on both priesthoods to his followers and successors.

But, unlike some of the more unique notions of Mormonism, the priesthood in the line of Aaron and the priesthood of Melchizedek are well established in biblical history. The Bible speaks concerning the past, present, and future of both priesthoods, but in neither case does it allow for their restoration to Joseph Smith and his associates in the 1800s.

The Aaronic Priesthood is the one discussed in Scripture to the greatest extent. It was first introduced when God called Moses to lead the nation of Israel out of Egyptian captivity. Besides telling Moses what his role would be, the Lord also gave an assignment to Moses' older brother Aaron, saying, "I know that he can speak well. . . . And he shall be thy spokesman unto the people." (Exod. 4:14, 16). Later, God formalized Aaron's position: "And take thou unto thee Aaron thy brother, and his sons with him, from among the children of Israel, that he may minister unto me in the priest's office" (Exod. 28:1). Much of the remainder of the books of Exodus and Leviticus consist of divine instructions concerning the priestly role of Aaron and his sons, their clothing, the sacrifices and ceremonies they would perform, and so on. The history of the Aaronic Priesthood is continued through the period of the judges and the reigns of the kings of Israel and Judah, right up until the time when the Jews were taken captive to Babylon. The kingdom in the family line of David ended then, and so did the priesthood in Aaron's lineage.

When the Jews returned after a generation or two of Babylonian captivity a form of priesthood was restored, but Israel's occupation by a succession of powers—Babylon, Persia, Greece, Rome—resulted in priests, and high priests in particular, who were political appointees rather than inheritors from Aaron. The Roman destruction of Herod's temple and deportation of the Jews gave the Aaronic Priesthood its final deathblow. Taken as prisoners of war and sold as slaves by the Romans, the Jews became like the black slaves in America who lost track of their ancestors' tribal roots. With genealogical records lost and tribal distinctions obscured, no Jewish man could claim to be an Aaronic priest, since the office depended entirely on inheritance. While Jews to this very day carry the family name Cohen, meaning "priest," none can validate a claim to the Aaronic Priesthood, and Jewish religious life is regulated by rabbis instead of priests.

God allowed the Aaronic Priesthood to terminate because it had fulfilled its purpose as part of the old covenant foreshadowing and leading up to the new covenant mediated by Christ. Acting as high priest of the new covenant by pouring out his own blood at the cross, Jesus Christ accomplished the forgiveness of sins that the repeated offering of animal sacrifices[5] by Aaronic priests only pointed forward to, but could not actually accomplish (Heb. 8:13; 9:1, 9–28; 10:1–8). "He taketh away the first, that he may establish the second. By the which will we are sanctified through the offering of the body of Jesus Christ once for all" (Heb. 10:9, 10). Thus, the Aaronic Priesthood with its sacrifices was taken away and replaced by the priesthood of Christ, who offered a final sacrifice once and for all. There will never again be a need to restore the Aaronic Priesthood.

Moreover, a comparison of what existed in Israel with the Mormon "Aaronic Priesthood" shows that the latter is in no way a restoration of the former. The Mormon claimants (1) are not from the family line of Moses' brother Aaron, (2) do not carry out the function of Aaronic priests outlined in the Bible books of Exodus, Leviticus, Numbers, and Deuteronomy, and (3) do not even worship the God of Israel, the one true God.[6]

As to Melchizedek, the Bible has much less to say. He is referred to only twice in the Old Testament: once historically in Genesis chapter 14, where he is presented as the priestly king of Salem to whom Abraham tithed a tenth of his war booty; and once prophetically in Psalm 110:4, which foretells that the Messiah would be "a priest for ever after the order of Melchizedek." In the New Testament the writer of Hebrews refers to Melchizedek throughout chapters 5, 6, and 7. He makes the point that the prophetic fulfillment is found in "Jesus, made an high priest for ever after the order of Melchisedec" (Heb. 6:20). And he states further that, "this man, because he continueth ever, hath an unchangeable priesthood. Wherefore he is able also to save them to the uttermost that come unto God by him, seeing he ever liveth to make intercession for them" (Heb. 7:24, 25). Since Christ was given the Melchizedek Priesthood forever, and continues to live and to carry on that priesthood, it makes no sense to speak of a restoration of the Melchizedek Priesthood in modern times.

Besides these facts about the Aaronic and Melchizedek priesthoods, the plain wording of Acts 3:20 and 21 speaks of the return of Christ and makes no mention of a restoration of ancient priesthoods in the modern Mormon Church.

See also the discussions of Genesis 14:18; Psalm 110:4; and 1 Corinthians 12:28.

Acts 7:55, 56

But he, being full of the Holy Ghost, looked up stedfastly into heaven, and saw the glory of God, and Jesus standing on the right hand of God, And said, Behold, I see the heavens opened, and the Son of man standing on the right hand of God.

Some Mormons may use this verse to attack the doctrine of the Trinity as well as try to prove that God the Father has a body like our own.

Their argument against the Trinity goes like this: Since Stephen saw two distinct personages, one standing next to the other, the Father and the Son must be two different Gods and not one divine person as trinitarians believe. The flaw in this argument is, of course, that it attacks a "straw man" Trinity rather than the concept of deity actually adhered to by orthodox Christianity. The traditional church teaching is that the Father is *not* the Son, and that the Son is *not* the Holy Spirit, yet these three distinct persons share the same divine nature and make up the one true God. But the rank-and-file Mormon has not had enough direct exposure to Christian theology to know this. When Mormons assert that trinitarians believe God to be a single person, they are misstating the Trinity doctrine. So when they proceed to disprove this concept by showing the Son to be distinct from the Father, they are actually knocking down a straw man that they themselves have set up—an effective debating technique, but not a sound refutation of Christian belief.[7]

As to their second use of Acts 7:55, 56, namely to try to prove that God the Father has a body resembling ours, it should be remembered that "No man hath seen God at any time" (John 1:18). What Stephen saw must have been a vision. And a vision does not necessarily portray someone in an actual physical appearance. This can be seen from the description of Jesus Christ in a vision the apostle John saw: "His head and his hairs were white like wool, as white as snow; and his eyes were as a flame of fire; And his feet like unto fine brass, as if they burned in a furnace . . . and out of his mouth went a sharp twoedged sword; and his countenance was as the sun shineth in his strength" (Rev. 1:14–16). Just as John's vision does not necessarily describe what Jesus actually looks like, Stephen's vision in Acts, chapter 7, does not necessarily portray God the Father as he actually is.

See also the discussions of Genesis 1:26, 27; 32:30; Matthew 3:16, 17; and Hebrews 1:3.

Acts 17:28, 29

For in him we live, and move, and have our being; as certain also of your own poets have said, For we are also his offspring. Forasmuch then as we are the offspring of God, we ought not to think that the Godhead is like unto gold, or silver, or stone, graven by art and man's device.

The apostle Paul said this to the men of Athens to turn them away from the worship of graven images. Mormons, however, focus on the term "offspring of God" and see in these verses a biblical confirmation of their belief in human pre-existence.

Footnotes to these verses in the Salt Lake City Bible refer the reader to: "TG [Topical Guide] Man, Antemortal Existence of" and "TG Man, a Spirit Child of Heavenly Father; Man, Physical Creation of; Man, Potential to Become Like Heavenly Father; Sons and Daughters of God; Spirit Creation." Mormonism teaches that heavenly parents begat spirit children in heaven; then, after they lived with them there for some time, they gave them bodies through birth as humans on the earth. All of us, according to this teaching, were spirit children of God before being born to our human parents.

But is that what Paul was teaching the men of Athens? No. Mormon doctrine was unknown to him. As a Jew converted to follow Christ, Paul was familiar with the Old Testament, but he had, of course, never seen the Mormon scriptures, particularly Doctrine and Covenants and the *Book of Abraham* that introduced these teachings in the mid-1800s. Such doctrines fall into the category of "another gospel" such as Paul warned the Galatian congregation against: "I marvel that ye are so soon removed from him that called you into the grace of Christ unto another gospel: Which is not another; but there be some that trouble you, and would pervert the gospel of Christ. But though we, or an angel from heaven, preach any other gospel unto you than that which we have preached unto you, let him be accursed" (Gal. 1:6–8).

Paul did not preach human pre-existence to the Galatians or to the men of Athens. In speaking of all humans as being "the offspring of God" he meant nothing more than what is stated in the Old Testament, namely that God created the first man and woman from whom all of us descended. Compare Isaiah 64:8: "But now, O Lord thou art our *father*; we are the clay, and thou our potter; and we all are *the work of thy hand.*" Also, Malachi 2:10: "Have we not all one *father*? hath not one God *created* us?" (Emphasis added.)

See also the discussions of Jeremiah 1:5; John 17:5; and Romans 8:16, 17.

Acts 20:30

Also of your own selves shall men arise, speaking perverse things, to draw away disciples after them.

This is one of several verses Mormons use in arguing that the entire Christian Church abandoned the true gospel of Christ and went into apostasy centuries ago, left no true church on earth, and necessitated the restoration of Christianity by Joseph Smith in the early 1800s. However, Acts 20:30 does not say that all of the disciples would follow such apostate teachers. And history records that men did arise and did draw disciples after themselves (in fact, it continues to happen today), but there is no record of a complete apostasy terminating the existence of true Christianity. Such an event would invalidate Jesus' promise that "I will build my church; and the gates of hell shall not prevail against it" (Matt. 16:18).

See also the discussions of Galatians 1:8; 2 Thessalonians 2:3; and 1 Timothy 4:1, 2.

Romans

Romans 8:16, 17

The Spirit itself beareth witness with our spirit, that we are the children of God: And if children, then heirs; heirs of God, and joint-heirs with Christ; if so be that we suffer with him, that we may be also glorified together.

Pulling these verses out of context, Mormons have been taught to see in them statements about humanity in general: that humans are all spirit "children of God" and, as such, can hope to become Gods themselves. One of the footnotes to these verses in the LDS Bible directs the reader through the Topical Guide to this passage of latter-day Mormon scripture: "Then shall they be gods, because they have no end; therefore shall they be from everlasting to everlasting, because they continue; then shall they be above all, because all things are subject unto them. Then shall they be gods, because they have all power, and the angels are subject unto them" (Doctrine and Covenants 132:20).

However, in thus interpreting Paul's words to the Romans, Mormons go beyond what he wrote regarding both children of God and exaltation.

Far from all mankind being spirit children of God, the immediate context shows that Christians become children of the heavenly Father by adoption (Rom. 8:15). Discussing the same thing in Galatians 4:5, 6, Paul again says that we become sons of God when we "receive the adoption of sons." An adopted child is not one originally or by nature. Contrary to the Mormon thought that people started out as children of God, the Bible shows that this adoption is something Christians receive when they come into a relationship with God through Jesus Christ (Rom. 8:8, 9, 15).

But even those who receive this adoption "that we may also be glorified together" with Christ do not become Gods as Mormon scripture teaches (Rom. 8:17). Joseph Smith elaborated, saying, "Here, then, is eternal life—to know the only wise and true God; and you have got to learn how to be Gods yourselves, and to be kings and priests to God, the same as all Gods have done before you" (*Teachings of the Prophet Joseph Smith*, p. 346). But the true God says clearly, "I am the first, and I am the last; and besides me there is no God" (Isa. 44:6); and, "understand that I am he: before me there was no God formed, neither shall there be after me" (Isa. 43:10).

The Bible teaches that people can become children of God by adoption, and that such ones receive exaltation in Christ, but it does not support the Mormon teaching that all people start out as children of God with the goal of becoming Gods themselves.

See also the discussions of Matthew 5:48; John 17:5; and Acts 17:28, 29; Nehemiah 9:6.

1 Corinthians

1 Corinthians 8:5

For though there be that are called gods, whether in heaven or in earth, (as there be gods many, and lords many).

Pulled from its context this verse may indeed seem to support the LDS Church doctrine of the plurality of Gods. But that is the danger of reading Bible verses out of context: they can be made to appear to teach something altogether different from what the passage in which they are found actually says.

Thus we find that the words quoted above are immediately preceded by the announcement that "there is none other God but one" (v. 4). And they are immediately followed by the declaration

that "to us there is but one God, the Father" (v. 6). Sandwiched
between these two solid statements of monotheism, it is illogical
to interpret verse 5 as though it proclaims polytheism.

What is actually meant, then, by the reference here to "many"
Gods? One step toward understanding it is to notice that the first
part of the verse says they are "called" gods. There is a difference
between *being* a god and being *called* a god. And just who are
being called gods in this discussion? Examination of the wider
context reveals that Paul is writing the Corinthian congregation
about food sacrificed to idols. In the mind of an individual who
worships an idol, the idol is a god. Christians, on the other hand,
"know that an idol is nothing in the world, and that there is none
other God but one" (v. 4).

But, while Christians know there is only one God, "there is not
in every man that knowledge" (v. 7). And persons without
knowledge of the one true God tend to worship idols and to call
their idols gods. Far from teaching the plurality of gods,
1 Corinthians 8:5 actually attributes such a belief to persons who
lack true religious knowledge.

See also the discussions of Psalm 82:1, 6 and John 10:34, as
well as chapter 2, "What the Mormon Church Teaches."

1 Corinthians 12:28

And God hath set some in the church, first apostles, secondarily
prophets, thirdly teachers, after that miracles, then gifts of healings,
helps, governments, diversities of tongues.

Mormons use this verse to support their claim that their
church organization is the same as existed in the primitive church
Jesus Christ established, that the LDS Church constitutes the
restoration of the original Christian church. But it is an easy matter for any religious sect to assign such titles as "apostle" and
"prophet" to positions within their organization; in fact, a number of other groups and denominations do the same thing.

Moreover, the Mormon Church fails to follow the first century
pattern accurately. As clearly stated above in 1 Corinthians 12:28,
apostles come first and prophets second, but the LDS organization has this reversed with prophets first and apostles second.

Also, the Mormons have fifteen apostles, a departure from the original pattern of twelve (Luke 6:13, Acts 1:25, 26).

In addition, from 1 Timothy 3:12 we learn that deacons are married with children, while in the present Mormon Church deacons are in the twelve-to-fourteen-year-old range. Few, if any, of these are married or have children.

Mormons cannot rightly claim that they follow the pattern of the primitive Christian church.

See also the discussions of Amos 3:7; Ephesians 4:11; and Hebrews 1:1, 2.

1 Corinthians 15:29
Else what shall they do which are baptized for the dead, if the dead rise not at all? why are they then baptized for the dead?

Much if not most of the activity in Mormon temples involves ceremonies for the benefit of the dead. Using information gleaned from elaborate and detailed genealogical research, vicarious baptisms and even marriages are performed with the idea that the dead people whose names are invoked actually benefit from these ceremonies just as much as if they were live participants. For biblical support Mormons turn to the verse quoted above.

First Corinthians 15:29 has been a mystery for apologists, with literally hundreds of different interpretations proposed. The reason for such ambiguity is obvious: the verse deals with a subject mentioned nowhere else in the Bible, yet does so without any introduction or explanation, as if it is expected that the reader will already know what is meant. And the members of the Corinthian congregation no doubt understood the reference. After all, even though it is titled "First Corinthians" in the Bible, this was not Paul's first letter to them (1 Cor. 5:9). He had spent time in Corinth and was familiar with both the church and the city. But we, never having lived in first-century Corinth or visited the church there, are left at a disadvantage.

Cults love to take verses like this and run with them, sometimes developing an extensive doctrinal framework on a single obscure passage. And even sincere Christians sometimes allow imagination to take over where knowledge stops. But sound interpretation must be based on what is known about the verse, its immediate context, and the wider context of Paul's letters and the rest of the Bible. On this basis commentators have come up with some plausible explanations. One writer thought that it could refer to people who promised dying Christian relatives that they would get baptized and then followed through on the promise after they died by in effect getting baptized for the dead persons. Others have suggested that some in the Corinthian congregation added the wrong practice of proxy baptism for the dead to their sectarian divisions (1 Cor. 1:10), their carnality (3:1), their immorality (5:1), their heresies (11:19), their abuse of the Lord's supper (11:21), and their misuse of spiritual gifts (ch. 12–14).

However, we think an explanation more in keeping with the rest of Paul's writings can be arrived at as follows. Notice that in 1 Corinthians chapter 15 the apostle Paul is teaching the Corinthian church about the resurrection of Christ, the resurrection of the dead, and the resurrection of the body. From verse 1 and throughout the whole chapter Paul addresses "brethren" in the Lord and speaks in terms of *you, we,* and *us,* with one exception. Only in verse 29 are *they* mentioned: "Else what shall they do which are baptized for the dead, if the dead rise not at all? why are they then baptized for the dead?" From this it would be reasonable to conclude that Paul talks in verse 29 about a group outside the Christian community. Baptism for the dead is not mentioned anywhere else in the Bible. If it were an ordinance of the church one would expect to see the teaching repeated and elaborated on.

Moreover, the time and effort Mormons devote to genealogy work in preparation for their practice of baptism for the dead in their temples seems to conflict with what Paul wrote in 1 Timothy 1:3, 4: namely, "Charge some that they teach no other doctrine, Neither give heed to fables and endless genealogies, which minister questions, rather than godly edifying which is in faith." It also violates the admonition of Titus 3:9 to "avoid foolish questions, and genealogies, . . . for they are unprofitable and vain."

If a Mormon remains unconvinced after seeing the above evidence, you may wish to show him an internal contradiction in his own religion. The following passages in the Book of Mormon teach that only in this life can we obtain salvation: 2 Nephi 9:38; 26:11; Alma 5:28; and Mosiah 16:5, 11; 26:25–27. Even more plainly, Alma 34:31–35 teaches that "*now* is the time and the day of your salvation. . . . For behold, this life is the time for men to prepare to meet God. . . . For behold, if ye have procrastinated the day of your repentance even until death, behold, ye have become subjected to the spirit of the devil, and he doth seal you his . . . and this is the final state of the wicked." We do not accept these statements in the Book of Mormon as authoritative, of course, but Mormons do. So they are left with the problem of reconciling their church's ordinance of baptism for the dead with their own sacred scriptures that rule out the practice.

1 Corinthians 15:40–42

There are also celestial bodies, and bodies terrestrial: but the glory of the celestial is one, and the glory of the terrestrial is another. There is one glory of the sun, and another glory of the moon, and another glory of the stars. . . . So also is the resurrection of the dead.

Mormons see in these verses confirmation of their belief in three heavenly destinations: the telestial kingdom, the terrestrial kingdom, and the celestial kingdom. Christ's atonement gave virtually all mankind general salvation which, in the Mormon view, means simply resurrection. Nonreligious people and even atheists are "saved" in this sense, but are resurrected to the lowest or telestial kingdom. Members of christendom's churches and other religious people who sought to please God but who never joined the LDS Church will be raised to life in the terrestrial kingdom. And faithful, obedient Mormons will reach the highest or celestial kingdom, where they may even become Gods.

These doctrines are taught in the "latter-day revelations" of Joseph Smith and other LDS leaders (particularly in Doctrine and Covenants, Section 76). But are they taught in the Bible, specifically in Paul's letter to the Corinthians? Not at all. A closer look at context and the words quoted above reveals that Paul was not talking about different kingdoms at all. Rather, he was talking about bodies. He was answering the question, "How are the dead raised up? and with what body do they come?" (1 Cor. 15:35). Using illustrations, he compared a seed planted in the ground to the body God gives the resulting plant. Next, he spoke of four different types of flesh: human, animal, fish, and bird (v. 39). Then he contrasted celestial (literally, *heavenly*) bodies with terrestrial (literally, *earthly*) bodies.[8] If there is any doubt as to what Paul meant by celestial or heavenly bodies, verse 41 clarifies it with examples: the sun, the moon, and the stars. Then Paul went on to develop the point he was illustrating, namely that the resurrection body is greater than the body in which we die: "It is sown in dishonour; it is raised in glory: it is sown in weakness; it is raised in power" (v. 43).

Paul was thus writing about bodies, not about kingdoms. He contrasted earthly (terrestrial) bodies with heavenly (celestial) bodies, but he did not in any way teach that heaven was divided into kingdoms called celestial, terrestrial, and telestial—the latter being a word Joseph Smith evidently coined himself.

See also the discussions of Matthew 5:48 and Romans 8:16, 17.

2 Corinthians

2 Corinthians 13:1

In the mouth of two or three witnesses shall every word be established.

Sometimes Mormons will use this verse, or others like it, to argue along these lines: At least two witnesses are needed to establish something as truth. The Bible is only one witness, so a second witness was needed. God provided the Book of Mormon as that second witness, thus establishing the gospel of Christ.

The principal flaw in this argument is that it fails to recognize that the Bible itself is actually a collection of sixty-six books by dozens of writers. If more than one witness is needed to establish the gospel of Christ, then we have Matthew and Mark and Luke and John and Paul, and so on, each of whom wrote separate testimonies on separate scrolls. It was only years later that the accounts written by these different individuals were assembled together and bound into a single volume as the Bible.

There is no basis for claiming that the Book of Mormon was needed as a second witness in addition to the Bible.

See also the discussion of Ezekiel 37:16, 17, and chapter 3, "Mormon Scripture."

Galatians

Galatians 1:8

But though we, or an angel from heaven, preach any other gospel unto you than that which we have preached unto you, let him be accursed.

Although this verse is more often used by Christians to challenge Mormonism, Mormons themselves will sometimes quote it in connection with their claim that the church set up on earth by Jesus Christ soon became apostate, teaching "another gospel," and so needed to be restored. The Protestant Reformation of the sixteenth century did not accomplish this, they assert, because the church was beyond reform. A total restoration was required, and this took place in 1830 when Joseph Smith founded the LDS Church.

It is true that another gospel was introduced early in the history of Christianity; that is what the apostle Paul wrote the Galatians about and warned them against (Gal. 1:6). From the rest of Paul's letter it appears that the other gospel being taught in Galatia had to do with salvation through works (compare Gal. 3:1, 2). Actually, there were a number of "other" gospels taught by persons who sought to "pervert the gospel of Christ" (Gal. 1:7). Some of these are mentioned specifically in the Bible: "the doctrine of Balaam," "the doctrine of the Nicolaitans," and the "doctrine" of "that woman Jezebel, which calleth herself a prophetess" (Rev. 2:14, 15, 20–24). The epistles of Paul, Peter, James, Jude, and John are full of warnings against false teachers and false teachings working their way into the church.[9]

But, did those other gospels succeed in penetrating the church to the point that the true gospel of Jesus Christ was lost and forgotten? No. In combating the counterfeit gospels, these Bible writers left us their inspired epistles outlining and defending the true gospel. Thousands of early manuscripts have survived to this day, preserving what they wrote. Controversies continued to disturb the church in the centuries that followed, but those disputes, too, are well documented with writings pro and con surviving for our examination. With church history so well preserved, it is possible for us today to trace the development of doctrines and practices over the years. We can follow the course of the debates over Gnosticism, Arianism, Sabellianism, and so on. Yet, in the mountains of manuscripts dating back nearly two thousand years, nowhere do we find evidence that the church originally taught anything resembling the "restored gospel" of Mormonism.

If it were true that the church founded by Jesus Christ originally taught such LDS doctrines as the plurality of Gods, men becoming Gods, celestial marriage, and God the Father having once been a man, and if it were true that those doctrines were later set aside in favor of what is now considered orthodox Christianity, there would certainly be some record of this. There would be very ancient Bible manuscripts containing those teachings that could be compared with later manuscripts leaving them out. And there would be writings pro and con debating those teachings, dating to the time when they were allegedly repressed. But no such evidence is available.

If the controversies over Gnosticism, Arianism, and Sabellianism generated such volumes of debate, certainly the changes Mormons believe took place in the early church would have resulted in some sort of paper trail. But, instead of ancient manuscripts, Mormons rely on the writings of Joseph Smith, who claimed to have received his information by direct revelation.

The evidence actually points to Mormonism being the "other gospel" and orthodox Christianity being the historically verifiable original gospel of Christ. Regardless of whether Joseph Smith received his information from an angel or from other sources, it still differs from what is recorded in the Bible. So the Scripture applies: "But though we, or an angel from heaven, preach any other gospel unto you than that which we have preached unto you, let him be accursed."

See also the discussions of Acts 20:30; 2 Thessalonians 2:3; 1 Timothy 4:1, 2; 1 Nephi 13:24–27; and the chapter 3, "Mormon Scripture."

Ephesians

Ephesians 4:11

And he gave some, apostles; and some, prophets; and some, evangelists; and some, pastors and teachers.

From Joseph Smith onward, each leader of the Church of Jesus Christ of Latter-day Saints has been designated a prophet. But, have they been true prophets, prophets of the true God? The Bible contains a simple test for separating true prophets from false prophets:

> But the prophet, which shall presume to speak a word in my name, which I have not commanded him to speak, or that shall speak in the name of other gods, even that prophet shall die. And if thou say in thine heart, How shall we know the word which the LORD hath not spoken? When a prophet speaketh in the name of the LORD, if the thing follow not, nor come to pass, that is the thing which the LORD hath not spoken, but the prophet hath spoken it presumptuously: thou shalt not be afraid of him (Deut. 18:20–22).

Have Joseph Smith, Brigham Young, and their successors as prophets in the LDS Church (1) spoken in the name of other gods, or (2) spoken prophecies that failed to come to pass? If either is the case, then the words of Deuteronomy 18:20–22 condemn them as false prophets. What do the facts show?

For examples of LDS prophets speaking in the name of gods other than the LORD (Yahweh or Jehovah), see the discussions of Genesis 1:26, 27; 2:7; Nehemiah 9:6; Daniel 7:9, 13, 22; and 1 Corinthians 8:5.

There are numerous instances of LDS prophets foretelling future events in which the thing prophesied "followed not nor came to pass." One example that any Mormon can find recorded in his own Scripture is Joseph Smith's prophecy concerning New Jerusalem:

> [The] city shall be built, beginning at the temple lot, which is appointed by the finger of the Lord, in the western boundaries of the State of Missouri, and dedicated by the hand of Joseph Smith, Jun., and others with whom the Lord was well pleased.
> Verily this is the word of the Lord, that the city New Jerusalem shall be built by the gathering of the saints, beginning at this place, even the place of the temple, which temple shall be reared in this generation ("Revelation given through Joseph Smith the Prophet, at Kirtland, Ohio, September 22 and 23, 1832," Doctrine and Covenants 84:3, 4).

Joseph Smith spoke those prophetic words in 1832,[10] over 150 years ago. That generation passed away without any Mormon temple being built in western Missouri, so the prophecy was false.

Mormons may attempt to defend Joseph Smith's prophecy by claiming that he intended the term *this generation* to have a meaning other than the customary one. They will use Mark 13:30 and Matthew 24:34 to support this. But *Joseph Smith—Matthew 1:34* (his version of Matthew 24:34 in the Bible, given in 1831) in the Pearl of Great Price says: "Verily, I say unto you, this generation, in which these things shall be shown forth, shall not pass away until all I have told you shall be fulfilled." This clearly shows that in Joseph Smith's understanding of the term "this generation," the clock would not start until the previously prophesied items occurred.[11] But the temple prophecy (D & C 84:3, 4) contained no contingent items that had to occur first. Even Smith's followers who lived within that generation understood him to mean their own lifetime. Thus, nearly forty years later Apostle Orson Pratt indicated that faithful Mormons were still waiting for the prophecy to come to pass:

> I hope this because God promised in the year 1832 that we should, before the generation then living had passed away, return and build up the City of Zion in Jackson county; that we should return and build up the temple of the Most High where we formerly laid

the corner stone. He promised us that He would manifest Himself on that temple, that the glory of God should be upon it; and not only upon the temple, but within it, even a cloud by day and a flaming fire by night.

We believe in these promises as much as we believe in any promise ever uttered by the mouth of Jehovah. The Latter-day Saints just as much expect to receive a fulfillment of that promise during the generation that was in existence in 1832 as they expect that the sun will rise and set to-morrow. Why? Because God cannot lie. He will fulfill all His promises. He has spoken, it must come to pass (Orson Pratt, May 5, 1870, *Journal of Discourses*, vol. 13, p. 362).

Apostle Pratt understood Smith to mean "the generation then living," and he expected to see a fulfillment before that generation passed away. However, in spite of his faith in Joseph Smith, the prophecy proved false. The Mormon Prophet failed the test of Deuteronomy 18:20–22.

Another Mormon defense is the argument that one error does not make Joseph Smith a false prophet. How many people does a man have to murder to be called a murderer? Only one. So, how many false prophecies does a prophet have to make to be a false prophet? The answer is obvious.

Lest someone claim that Smith made a single "mistake," another prophecy of his that failed to come to pass should be noted:

> I prophesy in the name of the Lord God of Israel, unless the United States redress the wrongs committed upon the Saints in the state of Missouri and punish the crimes committed by her officers that in a few years the government will be utterly overthrown and wasted, and there will not be so much as a potsherd left, for their wickedness in permitting the murder of men, women and children (Joseph Smith, May 18, 1843, *History of the Church*, vol. 5, p. 394).

The fact that the government of the United States is still standing, of course, makes this, too, a false prophecy.

Joseph Smith's successor, Brigham Young, also tried his hand at prophesying future events. For example, he foretold that the Civil War would not result in freeing the black slaves:

> Will the present struggle free the slave? No; but they are now wasting away the black race by thousands (Brigham Young, Oct. 6, 1863, *Journal of Discourses*, vol. 10, p. 250).

History proves this prophecy to be false; events did not follow or come to pass as Brigham Young said they would. Still, he persisted in prophesying:

> Do you think that we shall ever be admitted as a State into the Union without denying the principle of polygamy? If we are not admitted until then, we shall never be admitted (Brigham Young, August 19, 1866, *Journal of Discourses*, vol. 11, p. 269).

With the Mormon Church abandoning the practice of polygamy in 1890, followed by Utah's almost immediate admission to the Union as a state, this prophecy, too, proved false.

Numerous other examples could be furnished, but those listed above are sufficient to discredit the claim that Mormon "prophets" actually speak for God.

See the discussions of Amos 3:7 and 1 Corinthians 12:28.

2 Thessalonians

2 Thessalonians 2:3

Let no man deceive you by any means: for that day shall not come, except there come a falling away first, and that man of sin be revealed, the son of perdition.

Using this verse for support Mormons claim that there was a total falling away from Christianity early in church history. With no true church left on earth, it was necessary for Joseph Smith to restore Christianity early in the 1800s, they assert. However, they are reading into 2 Thessalonians 2:3 more than the verse actually says; it does not say that the falling away would be complete.

In fact, this teaching of a complete apostasy contradicts other Mormon teachings, such as the claim that three faithful Nephite disciples never died (3 Nephi 28:1–8) and the belief that the apostle John never died (Doctrine and Covenants 7:1–8). If those four believers remained, it could not be said that Christianity vanished from the earth.

Aside from those contradictory claims within Mormonism itself, what other evidence exists that there was never a complete and total falling away from Christianity that eliminated the Church from this planet? Believers in Jesus Christ will accept as strong evidence his promise that he would be with those taught "to observe all things whatsoever I have commanded you: and, lo, I am with you alway, even unto the end of the world" (Matt. 28:20). There would have to be some on earth following Jesus' teachings always, from the time of Christ to the end of the world.

See also the discussions of Acts 20:30; Galatians 1:8; and 1 Timothy 4:1, 2.

1 Timothy

1 Timothy 4:1, 2

Now the Spirit speaketh expressly, that in the latter times some shall depart from the faith, giving heed to seducing spirits, and doctrines of devils; Speaking lies in hypocrisy; having their conscience seared with a hot iron.

To a Mormon the many Bible passages foretelling false teachers and false teachings are all proof that true Christianity disappeared from the earth centuries ago and was restored by Joseph Smith in the early 1800s. However, such passages do not say that Christianity would disappear entirely, or that *all* would depart from the faith. Rather, as in the case of the verses quoted here from 1 Timothy, they predict that "*some* shall depart from the faith." But others kept the faith and kept preaching the true message of Christianity. As Peter promised, "the word of the Lord endureth for ever. And this is the word which by the gospel is preached unto you" (1 Peter 1:25).

See also the discussions of Acts 20:30; Galatians 1:8; and 2 Thessalonians 2:3.

Hebrews

Hebrews 1:1, 2

God, who at sundry times and in divers manners spake in times past unto the fathers by the prophets, Hath in these last days spoken unto us by his Son, whom he hath appointed heir of all things, by whom also he made the worlds.

Although Mormons are unlikely to bring up these verses for discussion, Christians can turn to them when Mormons attempt to argue that their church has authority by virtue of having a living prophet at its head. These words in Hebrews 1:1, 2 show that this was God's way of dealing with his people "in times past," prior to sending his Son. As Jesus himself explained it, "The law and the prophets were until John; since that time the kingdom of God is preached, and every man presseth into it" (Luke 16:16). God ceased to use prophets to lead his people when John the Baptist came and introduced the Son of God as the permanent head of the Christian Church.

See also the discussions of Amos 3:7 and 1 Corinthians 12:28.

Hebrews 1:3

Who being the brightness of his glory, and the express image of his person, and upholding all things by the word of his power, when he had by himself purged our sins, sat down on the right hand of the Majesty on high.

Mormons sometimes refer to this verse to "prove" that God the Father has a body of flesh and bones. "Otherwise, how could Jesus have sat down at God's 'right hand'?" they ask. However, in attempting to draw such a conclusion, they ignore the context and the scriptural use of this expression.

The Jewish/Christian audience addressed in the Epistle to the Hebrews knew that the right-hand position next to any ruler or king was a place of honor that carried with it great power and authority. We use a somewhat similar expression today when we speak of someone's right-hand man. If a historical account refers to Robert F. Kennedy as President John F. Kennedy's right-hand man, we do not therefore conclude that Bobby actually stood at Jack's right side.

Does Scripture here really make a similarly symbolic use of the expression "right hand"? Yes. The New Testament references to Christ as sitting at the right hand of God the Father all refer back to similar expressions in the Old Testament, most of them specifically to Psalm 110:1[12]: "The LORD said unto my Lord, Sit thou at my right hand." In fact, this verse is quoted in full in Hebrews 1:13: "But to which of the angels said he at any time, Sit on my right hand, until I make thine enemies thy footstool?" Note that two positions are spoken of here: (1) the right-hand position, and (2) the footstool position. If we agree that Christ's using his enemies as a "footstool" is not literal but rather symbolic of their being abased, then we are forced to admit that the first part of the same verse is symbolic of Christ's being exalted. With reference to God the Father, Jesus Christ, or any reigning king the Bible uses the right-hand position and the footstool position to represent exaltation and abasement, respectively. Since neither expression speaks literally of physical anatomy, the verses featuring such expressions can not properly be taken as proof that God the Father has a body like ours.

Hebrews 5:1, 4

For every high priest taken from among men is ordained for men in things pertaining to God, that he may offer both gifts and sacrifices for sins. . . . And no man taketh this honour unto himself, but he that is called of God, as was Aaron.

Authority is a central issue for Mormons. Having a living "Prophet" and Twelve "Apostles" at the head of their church, and the "restored" Aaronic and Melchizedek Priesthoods, they challenge traditional Christians and ask, "Where do you get your authority?"

The validity of the LDS claims to prophets and priesthoods is examined elsewhere in this book. See the discussions of Genesis 14:18; Psalm 110:4; Amos 3:7; Acts 3:20, 21; Ephesians 4:11; and Hebrews 5:6; 7:1.

But what of the charge that Christians outside the LDS Church lack authority from God? The Bible says, concerning Christ, that "as many as received him, to them gave he power to become the sons of God, even to them that believe on his name" (John 1:12). Such authority was given, not just to a few but to as many as received Christ; therefore, all believers receive authority from God. After warning of false teachers the apostle John writes: "But the anointing which ye have received of him abideth in you, and ye need not that any man teach you: but as the same anointing teacheth you of all things, and is truth, and is no lie, and even as it hath taught you, ye shall abide in him" (1 John 2:27). Individual Christians have a direct relationship with God by virtue of their anointing; they do not depend on a human authority structure over them.

Unlike the old Jewish covenant with its kings and priests, the new covenant mediated by Christ says to the whole Christian congregation: "Ye also, as lively stones, are built up a spiritual house, an holy priesthood, to offer up spiritual sacrifices, acceptable to God by Jesus Christ. . . . But ye are a chosen generation, a royal priesthood, a holy nation" (1 Peter 2:5, 9). And, "Jesus Christ . . . hath made us kings and priests unto God and his Father" (Rev. 1:5, 6). Whereas believers under the old covenant waited for the word of God to come to them through a priest or prophet, the new covenant says: "They shall not teach every man his neighbour, and every man his brother, saying, Know the Lord: for all shall know me, from the least to the greatest" (Heb. 8:11, quoting Jer. 31:34).

Rather than set up a powerful hierarchy and authority structure in his church, Jesus Christ left these instructions: "The kings of the Gentiles exercise lordship over them; and they that exercise authority upon them are called benefactors. But ye shall not be so: but he that is greatest among you, let him be as the younger; and he that is chief, as he that doth serve" (Luke 22:25, 26).

Hebrews 5:6; 7:1

As he saith also in another place, Thou art a priest for ever after the order of Melchisedec. . . . this Melchisedec, king of Salem, priest of the most high God, who met Abraham returning from the slaughter of the kings, and blessed him.

Mormonism teaches that the Church of Jesus Christ of Latter-day Saints contains the restoration of the Melchizedek Priesthood, and that this is one of the proofs that it is the one true religion. But the discussion of Melchizedek and priesthoods in Hebrews chapters 5 through 8 actually points to Jesus Christ, rather than to any modern organization on earth. The writer of Hebrews sums it up by saying: "Now of the things which we have spoken this is the sum: We have such an high priest, who is set on the right hand of the throne of the Majesty in the heavens" (Heb. 8:1).

See also the discussions of Genesis 14:18; Psalm 110:4; Acts 3:20, 21; and Hebrews 5:1, 4.

Hebrews 11:27

By faith he forsook Egypt, not fearing the wrath of the king: for he endured, as seeing him who is invisible.

To support Joseph Smith's claim to have seen God the Father, Mormons use this verse to "prove" that God is not really invisible to those who have been "quickened by the Spirit of God" (Doctrine and Covenants 67:11). But the verse does not say that Moses actually saw God. Rather, he "endured *as* seeing him who is invisible."

This verse is one of a long list that the writer of Hebrews presents as examples of the principle enunciated in chapter 11, verse 1: "Now faith is the substance of things hoped for, the evidence of things not seen." The point in Moses' case is not that he saw God but that through faith he was able to endure *as if* he had seen the invisible God. (Many modern translations render the Greek to say "as if" or "as though" rather than simply "as.") The principle illustrated by Moses and the others listed in Hebrews chapter 11, is the same as that stated elsewhere by Paul: "For we walk by faith, not by sight" (2 Cor. 5:7).

See also the discussions of Genesis 32:30; Exodus 24:10, 11; 33:11; and John 1:18; 6:46.

James

James 1:5

If any of you lack wisdom, let him ask of God, that giveth to all men liberally, and upbraideth not; and it shall be given him.

Rather than present a lot of "evidence" in support of the Book of Mormon's alleged authenticity, Mormon missionaries usually encourage their listeners to read selected chapters and then to "pray about the Book of Mormon." They say that God will answer the prayer of one sincerely asking whether it is true, and will confirm that the Book of Mormon is his inspired word. One of them may relate how God gave him a "burning in the bosom" when he himself prayed on the matter years earlier. The missionaries may add to James 1:5 this encouragement from Moroni 10:4 in the last chapter of the Book of Mormon:

> And when ye shall receive these things, I would exhort you that ye would ask God, the Eternal Father, in the name of Christ, if these things are not true; and if ye shall ask with a sincere heart, with real intent, having faith in Christ, he will manifest the truth of it unto you, by the power of the Holy Ghost.

Is it appropriate for Christians to follow the missionaries' advice to ask God whether the Book of Mormon is true? What could possibly be wrong with such a prayer? Scripture tells us that "There is a way which seemeth right unto a man, but the end thereof are the ways of death" (Prov. 14:12). And we remember that Satan, the devil, seemed to encourage Jesus to step out in faith when he tempted him to step off the pinnacle of the temple: "For it is written, He shall give his angels charge over thee, to keep thee: And in their hands they shall bear thee up, lest at any time thou dash thy foot against a stone." But Jesus answered him: "It is said, Thou shalt not tempt the Lord thy God" (Luke 4:10–12). So what seems like stepping out in faith, or praying in faith, may really be falling into a trap.

Suppose a man is about to embark on a certain voyage or on a particular business venture. To assure himself (or perhaps onlookers) that this course is God's will for him, he looks up to heaven and says, "Dear God, if what I am about to do is not your will, please strike me with lightning right now!" He closes his eyes for a moment, waiting. Then, since the blue sky produces no bolt to strike him, he looks up again and says, "Thank you, God, for showing me that this is indeed your will."

That man's "confirmation" from God is about as valid as that of a potential convert who prays about the Book of Mormon before going to bed and then receives the "burning in the bosom" the missionary had spoken of, thinking that this is God's way of saying the Book of Mormon is true, when actually it is something else.

While God encourages us to pray, he does not expect us to ask him questions that we ought to be able to answer for ourselves, or which he has already spoken through his Word the Bible, such as "Should I rob a bank?" or "Is *Snow White and the Seven Dwarfs* a true story?" And we cannot expect him to give us personal answers to such questions.

Then how should Christians evaluate the Book of Mormon? The same way that Jews in Berea evaluated the message preached to them by the apostle Paul: They "searched the scriptures daily, whether those things were so" (Acts 17:11). They compared what Paul preached with what the Old Testament said about the Messiah, and this solid evidence led them to accept Jesus as the Christ.

The Bible warns us, "Beloved, believe not every spirit, but try the spirits whether they are of God: because many false prophets are gone out into the world" (1 John 4:1). And we are encouraged to "Prove all things; hold fast that which is good" (1 Thess. 5:21). The passages discussed in chapter 6, "Verse-by-Verse Answers for Mormons—Book of Mormon," should suffice to try the Book of Mormon and to prove that it is not part of sacred Scripture.

See also the discussion of the Book of Mormon in chapter 3, "Mormon Scripture," and the discussions of 2 Corinthians 13:1.

1 John

1 John 4:12

No man hath seen God at any time. If we love one another, God dwelleth in us, and his love is perfected in us.

The King James Bible published by Mormons for their own use (Salt Lake City, 1990) features a footnote to this verse referring to the *Joseph Smith Translation* and giving its rendering: "No man hath seen God at any time, *except them who believe . . .*" [italics and ellipsis theirs].

For a refutation of this addition to the Bible, see the discussion of John 1:18, a text in which Smith made a similar change in his "translation," as well as the discussion of the Bible in chapter 3: "Mormon Scripture."

Revelation

Revelation 14:6

And I saw another angel fly in the midst of heaven, having the everlasting gospel to preach unto them that dwell on the earth, and to every nation, and kindred, and tongue, and people.

In Mormon eyes this is a biblical prophecy of the angel Moroni's visit to Joseph Smith. The LDS Church has taught its followers that "the everlasting gospel" is not proclaimed by the Christian churches, but rather that it disappeared from the earth soon after the death of Christ. And so it had to be restored by an angelic messenger. A footnote to Revelation 14:6 in the LDS Bible refers readers to the headings "Book of Mormon" and "Restoration of the Gospel" in the volume's Topical Guide. Under the latter heading in the Bible Dictionary is an explanation that there would be "a re-establishment of the gospel of Jesus Christ on the earth in the last days, with the powers, ordinances, doctrines, offices and all things as they have existed in former ages."

For a refutation of this doctrine see the discussions of Acts 3:20, 21; 20:30; Galatians 1:8; 2 Thessalonians 2:3; 1 Timothy 4:1, 2; and Hebrews 5:6; 7:1.

Revelation 22:18

For I testify unto every man that heareth the words of the prophecy of this book, If any man shall add unto these things, God shall add unto him the plagues that are written in this book.

Christians often show this verse to Mormon missionaries with the argument that they cannot accept the Book of Mormon because it is an addition to God's Word, in violation of this warning in the last chapter of the Bible. However, the missionaries are quick to point out that, although this verse is located at the end of our Bible, the books of the Bible are not arranged in strict chronological order. Genesis was likely written first and appears first in the Bible, but the other biblical books and epistles do not necessarily appear in the order in which they were written. And scholars generally agree that the book of Revelation was *not* written last; John's Gospel and his three epistles were probably written after Revelation. If John's Gospel could be added after the warning of Revelation 22:18, so could the Book of Mormon, the missionaries may argue.

Or, to avoid questions as to when John wrote his Gospel and epistles, they may simply turn to Deuteronomy 4:2 and read, "Ye shall not add unto the word which I command you, neither shall ye diminish ought from it, that ye may keep the commandments of the LORD your God which I command you." The Mormon missionaries will say, "There! If this prohibits adding the Book of Mormon it also prohibits adding the rest of your Bible after Deuteronomy."

The problem, of course, is due to misunderstanding of these verses in Revelation and Deuteronomy. Revelation 22:18 does not prohibit additional inspired writings; it is simply an injunction against adding to or subtracting from the Book of Revelation. It was perfectly proper for John to go on to write his Gospel and his epistles afterwards. But it was *not* proper for Joseph Smith to make changes throughout the Book of Revelation, as he did in the *Joseph Smith Translation*.

Deuteronomy 4:2, on the other hand, is a general injunction against adding to or subtracting from "the word which I command you," not thereby limiting God's expanding Scripture through additional inspired writings but telling us not to tamper with whatever God does provide in the way of Scripture.

While Revelation 18:22 does not relate directly to the Book of Mormon, Deuteronomy 4:2 does. Claiming divine inspiration for a volume that is actually the work of a man would amount to adding to the Word of God. For evidence as to whether or not this is true of the Book of Mormon, see chapters 3, "Mormon Scripture," and chapter 6, "Verse-by-Verse Answers for Mormons—Book of Mormon." See also the discussion of Deuteronomy 4:2.

6

Verse-by-Verse Answers for Mormons: Book of Mormon

Top Mormon leaders encourage their missionaries to use the Book of Mormon early in presentations to nonmembers. And potential converts who begin reading it find that it has a disarming effect. There are two reasons for this. First, it reads like a King James Bible and actually contains many passages taken directly from the Bible; and second, it surprisingly does *not* contain most of the unique teachings that make Mormonism significantly different from orthodox Christianity.

Major LDS doctrines *not* present in the Book of Mormon include the teaching that men can progress to become Gods, as God the Father allegedly did ("eternal progression"); that we were begotten as spirits by heavenly parents before coming to earth in physical bodies; that there are degrees of glory in the celestial heaven; that God the Father has a body of flesh and bones; that the Trinity is composed of three Gods, one in purpose; that there is a Heavenly Mother (the wife of God the Father); that God the Father has a father; that the birth of Christ resulted from a physical act of procreation between Mary and God the Father; and so on. Thus, the Book of Mormon gives only the "milk" of the LDS gospel and hence is more readily presented to nonmembers, but it does not give a true picture of Mormon doctrine as a whole. Therefore, Mormons do not normally turn to the Book of Mormon to defend these unique teachings of their church in discussions with outsiders.[1]

Still, Christians who know where to look can show them passages in the Book of Mormon that demonstrate it to be not the word of God but a blasphemous counterfeit. Familiarity with the verses discussed in this chapter may prove helpful in such encounters.

1 Nephi

1 Nephi 13:24–27

And the angel of the Lord said unto me: Thou has beheld that the book proceeded forth from the mouth of a Jew; . . . it contained the fulness of the gospel of the Lord of whom the twelve apostles bear record; . . . they have taken away from the gospel of the Lamb many parts which are plain and most precious. . . . And all this they have done that they might pervert the right ways of the Lord.

These verses are used by the Mormon Church to support its allegation that "plain and precious" parts have been lost from the Bible. Since even basic teachings concerning God the Father and Jesus Christ were allegedly lost or changed, a "restoration" was needed and was accomplished through Joseph Smith.

Although a full verification of the soundness and completeness of the Bible that has been passed down to us is beyond the scope of this book—indeed the evidence would fill many books—the Mormon attack on the Bible can be answered briefly in two steps.

First, since the claim that the Bible is incomplete rests largely on the above verses from the Book of Mormon, we can examine the reliability of *that* book as a witness against the Bible. Such an examination reveals that the Book of Mormon itself is of questionable origin and authenticity. Lacking credibility of its own, it is in no position to impeach the Bible. The discussions in this chapter on verses from the Book of Mormon and in chapter 3, "Mormon Scripture" demonstrate sufficient grounds for disbelieving what the Book of Mormon has to say about the Bible and about other matters.

The second step involves looking at the Bible itself and the basis for accepting it as reliable and complete. In contrast to the Book of Mormon, which is unsupported by history and archaeology, the Bible is verified by countless external histories and archaeological finds. Moreover, New Testament books quote from or attest to the validity of the Old Testament (Luke 24:44, 45; 2 Tim. 3:15–17; Heb. 4:4–7) and even other portions of the New Testament (Acts 1:2; 2 Peter 3:15, 16). Whereas the Book of Mormon lacks manuscript evidence, the Bible has been preserved in the form of thousands of manuscripts, in various languages, from various parts of the ancient world. And the Bible assures us of its preservation, saying, "The word of our God shall stand for ever" (Isa. 40:8; also 1 Peter 1:23–25).

True, the Roman Catholic Church adds certain apocryphal books to the sixty-six books accepted by Protestants, and there are additional books that others have argued for inclusion in the biblical canon. But this does not weaken the case for the Bible. Rather, it shows that even portions that some might say were removed are far from being lost. The portions excluded from sacred Scripture by early church councils are still available to anyone for examination and scrutiny.

In fact, the modern researcher can gain access to ancient manuscripts of canonical books and those judged noncanonical, as well as the texts of countless commentaries, discussions, debates, and arguments by writers both orthodox and heretical from the early centuries of the Christian church. With the early church fathers and opposers of Christianity debating the sacred writings and one another's writings, the volumes of such debate would certainly contain some record of any attempt to remove "plain and precious" parts of the gospel. But the Mormons have nothing to point to but the words quoted above.

A more thorough discussion of the completeness and reliability of the Bible can be found in such recent books as *Evidence That Demands a Verdict* by Josh McDowell and *The New Testament Documents—Are They Reliable?* by F. F. Bruce.

See also the discussion of Galatians 1:8.

1 Nephi 14:10

And he said unto me: Behold there are save two churches only; the one is the church of the Lamb of God, and the other is the church

of the devil; wherefore, whoso belongeth not to the church of the
Lamb of God belongeth to that great church, which is the mother
of abominations; and she is the whore of all the earth.

"Why do you attack us? We don't attack you." That is the familiar refrain raised by Mormons when they encounter Christians in
counter-cult ministry. (LDS missionaries may even cry "Persecution!" if you open your copy of *Mormons Answered Verse by Verse*
in their presence.) But, as the above quotation from the Book of
Mormon reveals, it was the Mormons who first attacked the
Christian churches. To members of the Church of Jesus Christ of
Latter-day Saints, theirs is "the church of the Lamb of God," the
only true church. The "other" church—embracing all non-Mormon
religions and therefore all Christian denominations—is "the church
of the devil . . . the whore of all the earth" in their view. If that does
not constitute an attack on Christian churches, what does?

When LDS missionaries are invited into a home and allowed to
present their series of prepared lessons, they begin making accusations against the churches very early in the course of those discussions. In relating Joseph Smith's alleged First Vision they repeat his
claim that heavenly visitors told him concerning the churches to
"join none of them, for they were all wrong . . . all their creeds were
an abomination in his [God's] sight; that those professors were all
corrupt" (Pearl of Great Price, Joseph Smith—History 1:19).

The missionaries also try to persuade their listeners to accept the
Book of Mormon as "another Testament of Jesus Christ", implying
that the churches have neglected or even suppressed part of the
inspired Word of God and have failed to preach the gospel of
Christ in its completeness. As the discussions continue, the missionaries present their standard argument that the gospel message
was lost around the end of the first century A.D. and needed to be
restored. The Protestant Reformation failed to accomplish this,
they say, and so it was left for Joseph Smith to begin this restoration by establishing the Church of Jesus Christ of Latter-day Saints.

When the young missionary elders complete their presentation,
the householder is left with the impression that the Christian
churches are a confusing array of squabbling denominations, all
misled by the devil, while the Mormon Church is the only true

church uniting all true believers under the headship of Christ. Must Christians remain silent in the face of such accusations and claims so as not to appear guilty of attacking Mormonism? No, Christians have the right—indeed the obligation—to "answer every man" (Col. 4:6; also, Heb. 5:14; Jude 3; 1 Thess. 5:21).

An honest answer includes the admission that not all is perfect in the churches. There are areas of weakness where criticism is valid. And a review of Christian literature reveals that Christians are not leaving it to the Mormons to provide such criticism, but rather that Christian leaders are constantly exposing error and wrong practices in their midst, just as the writings of Paul, Peter, James, Jude, and John focused attention on problems in the ancient churches of Corinth, Galatia, Ephesus, Thessalonica, Laodicea, and so on. In fact, the problems in today's churches are generally the same ones that troubled those first-century congregations, although perhaps manifested in a somewhat different form.

Yet, surrounded as it may be by personality problems and human weaknesses, the basic truth of Christianity is still found in the Bible and is still preached in Christian churches. But if Mormonism, on the other hand, proves to be "another gospel" or one that "would pervert the gospel of Christ," Christians are obligated to expose that fact just as Paul did when confronted with perversions of Christianity in his day (Gal. 1:6, 7).

Christ Jesus did not hold back from rebuking religious leaders who were "teaching for doctrines the commandments of men." He told them that their worship was "in vain" (Matt. 15:9). And Peter prophesied to Christians that "there shall be false teachers among you, who privily shall bring in damnable heresies" (2 Peter 2:1). If Mormon leaders are similarly teaching for doctrines heresies or commandments of men, it is appropriate for Christians to imitate Christ and Peter in exposing those falsehoods.

In thus "attacking" Mormonism, Christians are really just responding to Mormon accusations and speaking in "defense of the gospel" (Phil. 1:17).

1 Nephi 16:10, 16

And it came to pass that as my father arose in the morning, and went forth to the tent door, to his great astonishment he beheld

upon the ground a round ball of curious workmanship; and it was
of fine brass. And within the ball were two spindles; and the one
pointed the way whither we should go into the wilderness. . . . And
we did follow the direction of the ball.

According to this account Lehi found on the ground outside
his tent in the wilderness near Jerusalem what appears to be a
mariner's compass. In fact, the word "compass" is attached to it as
the story progresses (1 Nephi 18:12, 21; 2 Nephi 5:12; Alma
37:38). Footnotes in the Book of Mormon date the finding of this
compass at around 600 B.C. Yet non-Mormon historians tell us
that the magnetic compass was first used in navigation by the
Chinese around A.D. 1100 and that it appeared in Europe shortly
thereafter. Did a Jewish family actually find a compass seventeen
hundred years earlier, or is this an example of anachronistic error
in the Book of Mormon? We leave it for the reader to judge after
examining the evidence of anachronism in other verses. See, for
example, the discussion of 1 Nephi 18:25.

1 Nephi 18:25

And it came to pass that we did find upon the land of promise, as
we journeyed in the wilderness, that there were beasts of every
kind, both the cow and the ox, and the ass and the horse, and the
goat and the wild goat, and all manner of wild animals, which were
for the use of men.

Aside from the error of stating that oxen (*castrated* bulls) were
found roaming the wilds, the Book of Mormon also errs in locating some of these animals in the New World at all during the
sixth century B.C. For example, history and archaeology combine
to establish that full-sized horses were introduced to the Western
Hemisphere by Spanish conquistadors in the sixteenth century
A.D.[2]

Similarly, other passages in the Book of Mormon speak of steel
(2 Nephi 5:15; Ether 7:9), silk (Alma 1:29; 4:6), elephants (Ether
9:19), and wheat (Mosiah 9:9), even though the Smithsonian
Institution and prominent archaeologists state that none of these

were present in the New World during the Book of Mormon period of 600 B.C. to A.D. 421.

Like a felon found guilty of perjury, whose further testimony is not to be trusted, the Book of Mormon's inaccuracies concerning plants, animals, and material things call into question its purported history of peoples and nations.

For another example of anachronism in the Book of Mormon, see the discussion of 1 Nephi 16:10, 16.

1 Nephi 22:20

And the Lord will surely prepare a way for his people, unto the fulfilling of the words of Moses, which he spake, saying: A prophet shall the Lord your God raise up unto you, like unto me; him shall ye hear in all things whatsoever he shall say unto you. And it shall come to pass that all those who will not hear that prophet shall be cut off from among the people.

According to page notes in the Book of Mormon (Salt Lake City, 1990 edition) this was allegedly written "between 588 and 570 B.C." by a transplanted Israelite named Nephi who was reading from "the books of Moses," specifically Deuteronomy 18:15, 18, 19 (1 Nephi 19:23). However, the writer of the Book of Mormon mistakenly had him read this portion from Acts 3:22, 23 instead, even though the Book of Acts was not written until over six hundred years later.

Compare Moses' words of Deuteronomy 18:15, 18, 19 (KJV) with 1 Nephi 22:20, and then compare Acts 3:22, 23 (KJV). It is obvious which one is quoted in 1 Nephi.

For other examples of anachronistic quotation in the Book of Mormon, see the discussions of Alma 58:40 and Mormon 9:8, 9.

2 Nephi

2 Nephi 31:8, 10

Wherefore, after he was baptized with water the Holy Ghost descended upon him in the form of a dove. . . . And he said unto the children of men: Follow thou me. Wherefore, my beloved brethren, can we follow Jesus save we shall be willing to keep the commandments of the Father?

According to the page notes in the Book of Mormon these words were allegedly written "between 559 and 545 B.C." (Salt Lake City, 1990 edition). That would be nearly six hundred years before Jesus Christ was baptized and began his earthly ministry. Yet the past tense is used in verse 8, referring to Jesus' baptism as an event of the past, and verse 10 speaks to contemporaries about the need to "follow Jesus." This sort of gross anachronism, taken together with other evidence, points to the author of the Book of Mormon as a modern man living during the early 1800s; copying the style and even some of the words of the King James Bible he attempted to fabricate a similar account set in ancient America, but he made enough anachronistic errors to betray its true origin as a work of modern fiction.

For other examples of anachronism in the Book of Mormon see discussions of 1 Nephi 16:10, 16; 18:25; 22:20; Alma 58:40; and Mormon 9:8, 9.

Jacob

Jacob 2:26, 27

Wherefore, I the Lord God will not suffer that this people shall do like unto them of old. Wherefore, my brethren, hear me, and hearken to the word of the Lord: For there shall not any man among you have save it be one wife; and concubines he shall have none.

This passage poses a problem for Mormons. And well it should, since polygamy is one of the first things that come to most people's minds when the word Mormon is mentioned. In fact, some of the religious persecution that came upon the sect in the 1800s was occasioned not by its contradiction of Christian doctrine but by the practice of plural marriage among its members. Although Brigham Young insisted "It is not polygamy that men fight against when they persecute this people,"[3] it is easy to understand how men could be stirred up to mob action, fearing for their own women, after hearing reports—probably exaggerated—of Mormons marrying other men's wives and daughters.

Yet here we read that the Book of Mormon prohibits having more than one wife and strictly forbids having concubines. How, then, did Mormonism become almost synonymous with polygamy? Founder Joseph Smith claimed that he received a "revelation" from the Lord at Nauvoo, Illinois, which he put into writing on July 12, 1843, to the effect that plural marriage was God's will for his followers. The revelation is still part of Mormon scripture (Doctrine and Covenants, Section 132), but the practice continued as official LDS Church policy[4] only until September 24, 1890, when the church's fourth president Wilford Woodruff issued a manifesto commanding believers "to refrain from contracting any marriage forbidden by the law of the land."[5]

This latter development will remind many readers of the official declaration announced by recent Mormon president Spencer W. Kimball in June 1978, declaring that black men would henceforth be allowed to hold the priesthood in the church, a privilege that had always been denied them in the past. To outside observers, the success of the civil rights movement during the 1960s left the Mormon Church out of step with the rest of American society, and the decision to admit blacks to the priesthood was a move necessitated by adverse public opinion. But to believers it came as an official declaration from God through their leadership.

Was there a similar situation surrounding the abandonment of polygamy? Yes. History reveals that President Woodruff issued his manifesto just in time to avert political disaster.

Utah was part of Mexico when Mormons settled there in 1847. But the Treaty of Guadalupe Hidalgo, which ended the Mexican War in 1848, brought the Salt Lake City settlement back within the boundaries of the United States. In 1850 Congress established the Territory of Utah, refusing to admit it to the Union as a state because of the widespread practice of polygamy by its population. Repeated applications for statehood were turned down year after year for the same reason. And then during the 1880s Congress took the offensive, first passing the Edmunds Act in 1882, which disenfranchised all men who practiced plural marriage, and then in 1887 passing legislation dissolving the Mormon Church corporation and seizing much of its property. By 1890 Federal prosecutors had succeeded in using "gentile" juries to convict several hundred Mormon men of violating U.S. anti-polygamy laws, sentencing even prominent Utah officials to the penitentiary. Then, Church president Woodruff issued his manifesto and reversed the policy his sect's founder had instituted by "revelation" as an "everlasting covenant."

Today the LDS Church strictly forbids plural marriage, even expelling from membership any of the flock who are found practicing it. Yet it has been estimated that some 30,000 breakaway "fundamentalists" living mainly in the rural areas of western Canada, Utah, Arizona, Montana, California, and Mexico still follow Joseph Smith's "revelation" instead of Woodruff's. The Mormon Church, eager to clean up its public image, no doubt squirms in embarrassment whenever such diehard polygamous families come to the attention of the news media.

Christians can beneficially invite Mormons to turn to Jacob 2:26 and 27 and then review the above history with them. Ask why a church that claims to have been led by divinely inspired prophets since the 1830s would go against its own scripture to engage in polygamy for decades, abandoning the practice only when the full force of the United States government was brought to bear.

Some have seen in the practice of polygamy by Old Testament patriarchs an indication that God approved of it. But many of those ancient men also lied, cheated, murdered, committed adultery, and kept slaves. Such things are recorded in the Bible as historical facts, not as models to imitate. As to marriage, Jesus called men to return to the standard God made known "from the beginning" in the Garden of Eden, namely that *two* would marry and become one flesh (Gen. 2:24; Matt. 19:4–9). And the inspired qualifications for service in the Christian congregation state that "A bishop then must be blameless, the husband of one wife," and "let the deacons be the husbands of one wife" (1 Tim. 3:2, 12).

Mormons are accustomed to being challenged on the issue of polygamy. But they are also accustomed to being able to silence the objections of people who are armed with more rumor than fact. While the information presented above may not of itself cause a member to resign, it can add weight to a growing pile of evidence leading a sincere Mormon to re-examine the roots of his religion.

Mosiah

Mosiah 14:1

Yea, even doth not Isaiah say: Who hath believed our report, and to whom is the arm of the Lord revealed?

Many passages in the Book of Mormon are word-for-word copies of passages from the Bible, both Old Testament and New Testament. Here Mosiah 14:1 cites Isaiah and then proceeds to quote Isaiah 53:1. Mosiah 14:2 reproduces Isaiah 53:2; Mosiah 14:3 reproduces Isaiah 53:3; and so on through the end of the chapter. At first glance this may seem appropriate. But closer examination raises a number of revealing questions.

For example, why did Joseph Smith's "translation" read nearly word for word the same as the King James Version of the Bible? Compare Isaiah chapter 53 in various translations, and you will see that each translator has rendered it somewhat differently— which is only to be expected, since a thought written in Hebrew can be expressed in a number of ways in English. Yet Mormonism would have us believe that Joseph Smith translated "reformed Egyptian" characters into English and came up with almost exactly the same reading as the KJV translators working with Hebrew. This is all the more remarkable if we notice that when parts of Isaiah 53 are quoted in various books of the New Testament, the wording *varies* considerably, even in the New Testament of the King James Version itself.[6]

Could independent translators, starting with Hebrew on the one hand and with "reformed Egyptian" on the other, come up with English translations that read word for word the same? Yes, but the odds against it are astronomical. So the facts force the conclusion that Joseph Smith copied Mosiah 14 not from gold plates but from his King James Bible.

See also the discussion of 3 Nephi 13:14, 24.

Alma

Alma 58:40

They stand fast in that liberty wherewith God has made them free.

Bible readers will immediately recognize this as adapted from Paul's famous words in Galatians 5:1: "Stand fast therefore in the liberty wherewith Christ hath made us free." Yet the footnote in the Book of Mormon has the words being penned in the year 62 B.C., some time before Paul was even born.

For another example of anachronism in Book of Mormon quotations, see the discussion of 1 Nephi 22:20. For other instances where Joseph Smith copied inappropriately from the King James Bible, see the discussions of Mosiah 14:1 and 3 Nephi 13:14, 24.

3 Nephi

3 Nephi 13:14, 24

For, if ye forgive men their trespasses your heavenly Father will also forgive you; But if ye forgive not men their trespasses neither will your Father forgive your trespasses. Moreover, when ye fast be not as the hypocrites. . . . Ye cannot serve God and Mammon.

3 Nephi 13:14, 24 reproduces essentially word for word Matthew 6:14, 24 from the King James Version of the Bible. Yet Jesus is supposed to have spoken the words in 3 Nephi 13 during a visit to America in the year A.D. 34, whereas the message in Matthew 6 was part of the Sermon on the Mount he spoke in the land of Palestine a couple of years earlier. Would the Lord have repeated himself word for word like that, speaking in a different language to a different audience at a different time and place? And if he did, would a translation by Joseph Smith from "Reformed Egyptian" come out to be identical to the King James translation from Greek manuscripts, which in turn translated the Aramaic words Jesus used with his Jewish audience? The astronomical improbability of such a coincidence points to a much more reasonable explanation: Joseph Smith copied these words from his King James Bible.

See also the discussions of Mosiah 14:1 and Alma 38:40.

3 Nephi 15:17, 21, 22

That other sheep I have which are not of this fold; them also must I bring, and they shall hear my voice; and there shall be one fold,

and one shepherd. . . . And verily I say unto you, that ye are they of
whom I said: Other sheep I have which are not of this fold; them
also must I bring, and they shall hear my voice; and there shall be
one fold, and one shepherd. And they understood me not, for they
supposed it had been the Gentiles.

How should Jesus' words in John 10:16 be understood? For
Mormons there is no question as to the meaning, because chapters 15 and 16 of 3 Nephi in the Book of Mormon present Jesus
as repeating the words of John 10:16 and giving a detailed interpretation himself during an alleged visit in the year A.D. 34 to the
Nephite people of America.

As shown above, he allegedly teaches that the Nephites are the
"other sheep" referred to in John 10:16. But then the author of the
Book of Mormon commits a serious error of anachronism. He has
Jesus say that his listeners in Jerusalem thought Jesus was talking
about *the Gentiles* as "other sheep." True, the understanding of
John 10:16 as referring to the Gentiles was the view commonly
held by Christians in A.D. 1830 when the Book of Mormon was
published, and the writer of the Book of Mormon was evidently
attempting here to refute it. But there is no evidence that such a
view prevailed among Jesus' audience in Jerusalem. Neither the
unbelieving Jews nor the Jewish disciples of Jesus expected him to
gather Gentile disciples into his "one fold." In fact, when Gentiles
later began coming into the early Christian congregation, this was
met with surprise and even opposition (Acts 10:45; 11:1, 2). So
the author of the Book of Mormon commits an error of anachronism by locating in A.D. 34 an idea whose time had not yet come.

The discourse in 3 Nephi also mistakes the meaning of Jesus'
expression that his sheep would "hear my voice." It interprets this
in terms of literal, physical hearing, so that Jesus would have to
physically visit a locality for its people to be within range of the
sound of his voice. Jesus would not visit Gentile lands, so "the
Gentiles should not at any time hear my voice" (3 Nephi 15:23).
But Jesus did not mean "hear" in that sense. In John 18:37 he said,
"Every one that is of the truth heareth my voice," certainly not
meaning that he visited within sound range of everyone on the
side of the truth. Rather, this is hearing in the sense of believing:

"To day if ye will hear his voice, harden not your hearts" (Heb. 4:7). Thus in John 10:26 and 27 Jesus contrasts those who "believe not" and are "not of my sheep" with the statement that "My sheep hear my voice, and I know them, and they follow me." As the Bible presents it this is not a matter of which lands Jesus visited but of which human hearts are willing to "hear" and "believe."

See also the discussion of John 10:16.

Mormon

Mormon 9:8, 9

Behold I say unto you, he that denieth these things knoweth not the gospel of Christ; yea, he has not read the scriptures; if so, he does not understand them. For do we not read that God is the same yesterday, today, and forever, and in him there is no variableness neither shadow of changing?

Yes, we too can read those same expressions in the Scriptures: "the same yesterday, and today, and for ever" (Heb. 13:8) and "no variableness, neither shadow of turning" (James 1:17). Yet how was the speaker in the Book of Mormon able to "read" them in ancient America from the New Testament that had not yet been brought to this continent? A more likely explanation is that the Book of Mormon was written in the early 1800s as a work of fiction by a modern author who borrowed freely from the Bible but, in this case, forgot to keep his chronology straight.

Mormons may point out that the expression "the same yesterday, today, and forever" also appears at 1 Nephi 10:18, allegedly written a thousand years before Mormon 9:9, and so the speaker could have been quoting from 1 Nephi rather than from Hebrews. But that still leaves the quotation from James unresolved. Besides, there are enough other examples of anachronism and inappropriate use of biblical material in the Book of Mormon to convince an unbiased examiner that it is not an ancient work. For examples, see the discussions of 1 Nephi 22:20 and Alma 58:40.

It should also be pointed out that this verse contradicts the present day Mormon Church teaching that God was once a man and progressed to being a God.

Ether

Ether 1:33–37

Which Jared came forth with his brother and their families, with some others and their families, from the great tower, at the time the Lord confounded the language of the people, and swore in his wrath that they should be scattered upon all the face of the earth; and according to the word of the Lord the people were scattered. . . . He did not confound the language of Jared; and Jared and his brother were not confounded. . . . Their friends and their families also, that they were not confounded.

Here the Book of Mormon teaches that a man named Jared, his brother, and their families and friends were exempt from the confounding of language at Babel. The Jaredites left Babel and were the first people to inhabit the Western Hemisphere, but they eventually incurred God's wrath and killed each other off, leaving the land empty once again (Ether, chapters 1 through 15). But notice that the Bible says in Genesis 11:7, 9 that "the LORD did there confound the language of all the earth" so that "they may not understand one another's speech." This use of the word *all* makes it clear that there were no exceptions. God confounded *everyone's* language and scattered everyone. The story of the Jaredites contradicts the Bible.

Ether 15:29–31

Behold Shiz had fainted with the loss of blood. And it came to pass that when Coriantumr had leaned upon his sword, that he rested a little, he smote off the head of Shiz. And it came to pass that after he had smitten off the head of Shiz, that Shiz raised up on his hands and fell; and after that he had struggled for breath, he died.

Were the Book of Mormon an actual history book its stories would be true to life and death. But the account concerning Shiz could not possibly be an historically accurate description of a man's death. Once he had fainted from blood loss due to earlier wounds and had then, lying unconscious, been decapitated, a man would not after all this be able to raise himself up on his hands, fall down, and then struggle for breath. The story was clearly a product of the writer's imagination; it is not medically possible.

Moroni

Moroni 10:4

And when ye shall receive these things, I would exhort you that ye would ask God, the Eternal Father, in the name of Christ, if these things are not true; and if ye shall ask with a sincere heart, with real intent, having faith in Christ, he will manifest the truth of it unto you, by the power of the Holy Ghost.

Mormon missionaries encourage their listeners to pray about the Book of Mormon. They suggest that God will answer the prayer of one sincerely asking whether the Book of Mormon is true, and will confirm that it is his inspired word. Recognizing that their listener does not yet accept the Book of Mormon as authoritative, they also turn to the Bible and cite James 1:5 as reason to offer such a prayer: "If any of you lack wisdom, let him ask of God, that giveth to men liberally, and upbraideth not; and it shall be given him."

Is it appropriate for Christians to follow the missionaries' advice and ask God whether the Book of Mormon is true? See the discussion of James 1:5.

7

Some Techniques for Sharing the Gospel with Mormons

The best techniques to use in speaking with Mormons will depend on what you want to accomplish, how much time you have, and what you are able to invest. But, isn't your goal always to lead them to Christ, and aren't you obligated to invest whatever it takes to accompish that? Yes, of course, but circumstances will vary. For example, you may speak on one occasion to a young missionary who knocks at your door and very early in the conversation tells you that this is his last week in your community, he will be taking a plane back to Utah on Friday, and he can't wait to see his fiancée back home. On another occasion you may speak to a new employee at your place of work who has just been assigned to work alongside you on a two-year project, and whom you discover to be a Mormon.

In the first instance it will be your only opportunity to talk to the young missionary. It's now or never. In addition to the time factor, your visitor has a lot on his mind. Even if you present it well, a complex theological argument may not register because he is preoccupied with thoughts of flying home and seeing his sweetheart. In this case you will need a conversation that is brief and to the point, yet powerful and bold. Be loving, polite, and patient, but also be bold and clear in your presentation, because you will have only one chance to plant a seed, unless you obtain an address for future correspondence. Share your testimony and what it means to have Jesus in your life. Finally, before he leaves, you may want to pull from the shelf next to your front door a tract written especially for Mormons, and stuff it into his jacket pocket. (Every Christian should keep next to the front door a well-marked Bible and other appropriate materials for use when Mormons or Jehovah's Witnesses knock.) If you've managed to explode one or two of the beliefs he grew up with—taken the edge off his testimony—he may be forced to think about it on the way home. Or, to relieve the boredom of the long flight he may pull the tract from his pocket and read it.

If you try the above approach on your new workmate, you may give him or her something to think about, but he or she will probably go straight to the boss and request to be transferred as far away from you as possible. And the boss will probably ask why you spent an hour and a half of company time talking religion.

In the case of a fellow employee, relative, neighbor, or close friend you see on a regular basis an entirely different approach is called for. First, build rapport and credibility. Let your Christian manners and lifestyle speak for you. Talk modestly about your relationship with the Lord, and show a mild, friendly interest in your Mormon associate's religion. Ask questions that reflect curiosity rather than hostility or condemnation. To some extent a Mormon will feel obligated to assume the role of official spokesman when representing the church to an outsider, but the more informal and relaxed you can make the circumstances, the more likely you will be able to truly communicate rather than simply exchange clichés.

On the other hand, if you start off openly attacking the Mormon Church or obviously attempting to convert your friend, you will likely trigger a defensive reaction. And the stronger your attack or the more vigorous your conversion attempt, the greater will be the reaction you provoke. If you come to be viewed as a real enemy of the church, that may mean an end to communication with the individual, or at least an end to communication on religious subjects. So, when dealing with a Mormon you see on a regular basis, it is best to take a long-range view of matters; saying less now will allow you to say more in the long run.

Unless you have Mormon relatives or neighbors, your encounters will most likely be with missionaries. They usually travel in pairs and introduce themselves as "Elder so-and-so," but far from being elderly they are most often clean-cut young men recently out of high school. Forbidden to perform secular work while in missionary service, yet not supported by the LDS Church,[1] the young men depend on their personal savings and on family and friends for support—which explains why they often ride bicycles.

When LDS missionaries visit, you have to decide whether to give them an all-out presentation of the gospel on the spot, which almost guarantees they will not return, or to opt for prolonged discussions over a number of visits. To use the latter approach you must allow them to do most of the talking and to give their prepared presentations. This keeps them coming back each week. But at the end of each session tell something about what Jesus Christ has done for you and ask a question or two about failed Mormon prophecies, about doctrinal reversals, about Brigham Young's teaching that Adam is God, and so on—questions they cannot answer then but will have to research before their next visit. Some missionaries in this way have been given more troubling facts to think about than if they had been bombarded with information on one visit.

The only drawback to this slower approach is that instead of Elder A and Elder B returning for a second discussion, Elder A may return with Elder C. Then Elder C and Elder D come the following week, and so on. This allows you to present information to more of them, but makes it difficult to bring matters to a head with any of them. This would be a problem if the task of getting them out of Mormonism and into biblical Christianity were left completely up to you. However, the situation is more like Paul described in 1 Corinthians 3:6: "I have planted, Apollos watered; but God gave the increase." If you plant a seed with a young Mormon but never see him again, you can trust that another Christian down the road will water, and then another, "For we are labourers together with God" (v. 9). He directs the work and uses us and others to get the work done.

As indicated above, there is no set formula for witnessing to Mormons. Each witnessing opportunity is unique, and you must depend on the Holy Spirit to guide you and direct you. But there are some basic principles you can apply, things you should or should not do, and knowledge you should have or should gain. It will not be easy and indeed it may be very frustrating, but you should do it anyway.

Keep in mind that the ultimate goal is to lead Mormons into a personal relationship with the one true God of the Bible. Also note, they think they already are worshipping the one true God. It's up to you to show them that they have a different God, a different Jesus, another gospel, and that they are breaking the first commandment. The strategy is to first undermine the Mormons' testimony and confidence in the LDS organization—its teachings, official history, unique scriptures (Book of Mormon, Doctrine and Covenants, and Pearl of Great Price), and biblical misinterpretations. Your skills are important in selecting and presenting the information. The Mormons must become "teachable." Until they are, it is usually best to stay away from biblical proofs; such discussions easily turn into unprofitable scripture bashing.

In any case, depend on the Holy Spirit to guide you. Before you witness, here are some basics you should know.

1. Know what the Bible says about witnessing.
   See Ezekiel 3:18, 19; Matthew 28:19, 20; 1 Peter 3:15; 2 Timothy 4:2–4; Hebrews 5:14; Jude 1:3.
2. What do you need to witness to a Mormon?
   First, have a desire born of God. See Zechariah 4:6. Prayer is a powerful tool when witnessing. Use it regularly.
   Second, be a strong Christian yourself. Have a personal relationship with God and be familiar with the biblical foundation of your own beliefs.
   Third, know at least a few of the very unique non-Christian teachings of the Mormon Church.
3. Other factors to consider:
   Do not try to witness if you are a baby Christian spiritually, especially not to LDS missionaries; remember,

they have been thoroughly trained in the art of witnessing to you.
Never be rude or ridicule their beliefs. Always be polite
and patient.
Love them. Let the love of Christ show in you.

In summary, always use L.P.P.Q.: *L* is for *love*, *P* is for *patience*
and *politeness*, and *Q* is for *quality* of your presentation techniques
and the information you use. Use only factual information and
not hearsay. This is very important. Also, remember that your
issue is with Mormonism, not Mormons.

Is it proper for you, a Christian, to hide the fact that you are
attempting to get a Mormon out of the LDS Church and into biblical Christianity, and in so doing to ask questions that you already
know the answers to? There are numerous biblical examples of
God the Father and Jesus Christ doing this. See Genesis 3:8–13;
Luke 22:48; and John 18:4. Jesus used such questions in his teaching ministry, and you can copy his effective example.

You ought also to be aware of the techniques that Mormons
use in their attempts to win others to their belief system. They,
too, study how to present themselves effectively and how best to
overcome prejudices against their strange doctrines. Many of
them will pass beyond the "go slow" approach and attempt to
deny or cover up some of their more bizarre teachings, justifying
this course by their concern for people like you who are "not
ready" to encounter their concepts. For example, when one
Christian householder asked a missionary whether he believed in
only one God, the young Mormon answered enthusiastically in
the affirmative. Yes, he believed in just one God.

"You don't believe in many gods?" the Christian asked again.

"No! Just one God, the same as you believe," came the reply.

But this householder was an informed Christian and knew to
press the issue further by asking, "Do you mean to say that you
believe there is only one God in all the entire universe?"

Now the Mormon began fidgeting nervously. Looking down at
his feet he admitted, "Well, no. We believe there is just one God
for this planet. Naturally, other planets have their own gods. I
thought we were just talking about this planet."

This demonstrates that Mormons sometimes talk with their fingers crossed, so to speak. Not intending to harm you but rather to bless you through conversion to the true church, they may hold back certain information while at the same time supplying other information that is actually misleading. This may take the form of using familiar words with different meanings, as in the case of the young missionary who claimed to believe in only one God. He saw himself not as lying but as going out of his way to help the Christian by avoiding offensive language or concepts.

Notice, too, the teaching methods that Jesus used. Glancing quickly over any one of the four Gospel accounts, you will observe that many of his sentences had question marks at the end. Question marks are shaped like hooks (?) and they can hook onto answers and pull them out through the other person's mouth. Jesus was highly skilled at using these "hooks." Rather than shower his listeners with information he used questions to draw answers out of them, thereby causing them to think about the subject. A person can close his ears to facts he doesn't want to hear, but if a pointed question causes him to form the answer in his own mind, he can't escape the conclusion, because it's a conclusion he has reached himself.

Generally speaking you should ask only questions that you already know the answers to and can document. This is important, because (1) the Mormon may not really know the correct answer, or (2) the Mormon may purposely evade the correct answer. But, knowing the answers yourself, you can ask supplementary questions to teach him the facts or to smoke out knowledge that he is concealing. For example, if you ask whether a Prophet of the LDS Church ever taught that Adam was God, and the Mormon either denies it or claims not to know, you can then go on to ask more specifically about Brigham Young, inquiring about references to this teaching in his writings. (See the discussion of Daniel 7:9.)

It takes patience to draw answers from the Mormon rather than provide them yourself. But if you provide the answers, the effect can be quite different. For example, you can tell a Mormon, "You have been deceived. The LDS Church is a false prophet. You need to get saved." But if he has not yet reached those conclusions in his own mind, he is likely to become offended and to reject whatever else you have to say. If you want him to reach those conclusions, you must lead his thinking in that direction.

Rather than comment, "Look at what Isaiah says in chapter 44, verses 6 and 8. He says that no other gods exist, besides the LORD," you would do better to ask the Mormon to read the verses aloud, and then ask, "Whom do you think the writer was referring to in this verse? What did he say about him?" The Mormon may not say the right answer out loud, but you will see his facial expression change when he gets the point.[2]

This volume contains plenty of ammunition for waging spiritual warfare against the bastion of Mormonism. But if the Christian warrior corners an individual Mormon and lets him have it with both barrels in rapid-fire succession, the result is likely to be disappointing. The Mormon leaders themselves know that the human mind can absorb only so much information at one time, and so they instruct missionaries to plan on spending several months with people they are trying to convert. Even an inexperienced Mormon would know better than to bombard a "Gentile" with the deeper and more exotic teachings, "the meat of Mormonism," on the first visit. And the Mormons are correct in their techniques, one reason for the amazing growth of their organization. So, we do well to learn from them about effective methods.

Jesus knew how much his listeners would be able to absorb at one time, and therefore did not try to overfeed them. Even after he had spent many months with the apostles, he told them: "I still have many things to say to you, but you cannot bear them now" (John 16:12 NKJ). The gospel consists of both "milk" and "solid food" (Heb. 5:12–14). If you give solid food too soon to a baby, he will choke on it and spit it out. Realizing that it may take a long time for a Mormon to unlearn false LDS doctrines and relearn Bible truth, you should not give him too much to digest at one time.

Above all, your hope for success should rest in the Lord rather than in yourself, no matter how much preparation and study you may have done. "(For the weapons of our warfare are not carnal, but mighty through God to the pulling down of strong holds;) Casting down imaginations, and every high thing that exalteth itself against the knowledge of God, and bringing into captivity every thought to the obedience of Christ" (2 Cor. 10:4, 5).

8

Testimonies of the Authors

John R. Farkas

It is an early morning late in February 1984. As usual I am reading the scriptures while eating breakfast.

I am in the Book of Mormon, 1 Nephi 18:25. The verse mentions the cow, ox, ass, horse, goat, and wild goat. This morning is a little unusual, though, in that I find myself questioning how some of these animals could have been in the New World.

Didn't the experts say that full-size horses were not in the New World until the European explorers and settlers arrived? This thought had occurred to me at least once before, I think while I was investigating the Church of Jesus Christ of Latter-day Saints, the Mormons or LDS as it is usually called.

But this time the questions stayed with me and I found myself thinking about other questions that I apparently had suppressed in the past. I now had become teachable and open, a necessary prerequisite to receiving productive witnessing.

I didn't recognize it then, but for about the previous four to six months my testimony had shifted. It didn't, as it once had, include Joseph Smith and the Book of Mormon.

Starting with the late February period when I questioned the presence of certain animals in the New World, and continuing for about two months, I seldom had a complete night's sleep. Almost every night I woke up to study for one or two hours, in addition to using all of my free time for the same thing.

By the end of February I had shared my doubts with my resident Mormon expert, my born-again Christian wife, Phyllis. In 1975, when I had joined the LDS Church, she became a Christian and started her Mormon studies.

I had gone on to become the Elders Quorum President of the Fairport Ward (1981–1984), and in early 1984 of the newly reorganized Rochester 1st Ward, both in the Rochester, New York Stake, while Phyllis became an expert in Mormon studies and acquired a very extensive library. When I asked her for certain information, most of the time I had it within minutes.

By March 15 I had made up my mind to leave the Mormon Church. I knew it when I woke up that night and removed my temple garments.[1] I felt free!

But my drive to study and learn continued, this time to grow in depth and breadth in Mormon studies and about the Bible and Jesus Christ.

On March 20, 1984, I sent Stake President Dale Dallon my letter of resignation. The reasons I noted in my letter were: changes in the *Book of Commandments* versus Doctrine and Covenants; changes to the Book of Mormon; conflicts in early and present-day teachings; the translation of the *Book of Abraham*. I stated that "Joseph Smith was a fraud and has pulled off one of the greatest hoaxes ever!!!" My name was formally taken off the church rolls at a church court on May 10.

How did I get involved with the Mormon Church? It was my wife's fault, so I now say, partially in jest.

In 1974 when I became concerned with the food supply chain and saw a need to have a long-term supply of food at home, Phyllis said, "The Mormons do that sort of thing. I'll send them a letter in Salt Lake City." Well, she did, and the LDS missionaries brought the answer to us. We both took the missionary lessons. I joined in July 1975; Phyllis became a Christian.

During that time I asked a very significant question without realizing how significant it was. I said to Phyllis, "If we are both praying to the same God, how come we are getting different answers?"

Now I realize that the Mormon gods are not of the Bible. Mormonism is *not* Christian.

When I left the Mormon Church on March 15, I was left essentially with the beliefs that I had held in 1974 before I joined the church. I was still a spiritual infant.

I believed in a supreme being, a God, but I did not accept the Bible as the Word of God and I did not accept Jesus Christ as his Son and my Savior.

I had a desire to know, so I studied the Bible, books about the Bible, associated with Christians, attended Christian Sunday services and Sunday school. Through this I came to know that the Bible is the Word of God and to know the real Lord Jesus Christ.

But even at this point I didn't know I was "saved."

Only after prayerful reading of John 3:16 with my friend Ross Amico—the director of a group that was to become Berean Christian Ministries, an organization dedicated to exposing cults—did I fully realize the truth of John 3:16 and that I was the "whosoever" mentioned in this verse. The promise that I could claim was the important thing.

Ironically, I accepted Jesus in the Palmyra, New York, Christian church that is adjacent to the Mormon chapel where I had been baptized nine years earlier *to the very week.* On Sunday, July 19, 1984, I answered an altar call at a local Christian church and made public my faith in the real Lord Jesus Christ. Now I know of the simplicity and beauty of his gospel.

I also had a drive to share my new-found knowledge and faith with others, Mormons and non-Mormons. It is interesting that I never had anything like this drive to share Mormonism with non-members. I was not a good member missionary.

In fact, in my last four to six months of church membership my feelings against missionary work surfaced. This became evident to me as my bishop attempted to increase missionary activity in our ward, and I only gave him passive support; but I didn't understand it then.

The Mormon people are a great people. They and their church have many characteristics that I found appealing. They are hard-working, conservative, successful, well organized, and they give great socials. They are good people in a worldly sense and should have the real Jesus Christ of the Bible.

Using the Bible, they present some convincing arguments that appear to support their doctrine. It is important for Christians to know the Bible and to know the real Lord Jesus Christ. A weak Christian is no match against the Mormon story; it is very appealing. Hence it is easier to keep people out of the Mormon Church than to get members out.

Groups like Berean Christian Ministries and Comments from the Friends perform a multi-function service in combating the false non-Christian teachings of the Mormon Church and similar groups. They help to educate Christians, Mormons, and others; they organize activities that individuals could not handle; they provide support for those trying to get out from under the Mormon story and similar organizations.

For over five years I have coordinated the Berean Christian Ministries outreach at the Mormon "Hill Cumorah Pageant" held annually in July near Palmyra, New York. It is the largest outdoor pageant in America, and up to 100,000 people attend each year. Over 13,000 pieces of Christian literature have been distributed each year.

I am a graduate of the University of Connecticut with a B.S. in mechanical engineering, and am a licensed New York State professional engineer. From 1962 to 1991 I worked at Xerox Corporation as a project engineer and a project engineering manager. I live with my wife, Phyllis, who is editor of *The Berean Report*, in Webster, New York.

One of the reasons I share the items in this last paragraph with you is to illustrate that worldly accomplishment and intellectual capability are different from spiritual capability. I have often been asked how a person could believe Mormon doctrine, and I can understand why the question is asked. But when the Mormon missionaries came to our house, I was a spiritual baby, and they only taught the milk of the Mormon "gospel." The meat comes later. As in Hebrews 5:14, I was not "of full age": "But strong meat belongeth to them that are of full age, even those who by reason of use have their senses exercised to discern both good and evil." I was not able to discern the real gospel of Jesus Christ from the "gospel" the Mormon missionaries had.

But through prayers of concerned Christians and my wife, who also had the perseverance and drive to put up with a rough situation, I became teachable and then "of full age." I hope and pray that the biblical Jesus Christ is your Lord and Savior as he is mine.

David A. Reed

My early religious training was in a big, white Unitarian church in rural New England south of Boston, where, at age fourteen, I concluded that religion was "the opium of the people." Later I went on to Harvard University and found that such atheism was perfectly acceptable there. By the time I was twenty-two, however, I came to realize that godless evolution offered me only a pointless existence in a meaningless universe, followed by a "dead" end. I began to think about God again.

At that time a Jehovah's Witness was assigned to work alongside me at my job, so I began asking him questions about his beliefs. His answers amazed me. It was the first time that I had ever heard religious thoughts presented in a tight-knit logical framework. In no time I became a very zealous Witness myself, and remained in the Watchtower organization for thirteen years serving as a full-time minister and a congregation elder.

I married Penni Scaggs, who was raised in the organization and was also a zealous Witness. Between the two of us we conducted home Bible studies with dozens of people, and brought well over twenty of them into the sect as baptized Jehovah's Witnesses. What interrupted this life of full dedication to the Watchtower Society? In one word, *Jesus*. Let me explain.

When Penni and I were at a large Witness convention, we saw a handful of opposers picketing outside. One of them carried a sign that read, "Read the Bible, Not the Watchtower." We had no sympathy for the picketers, but we did feel convicted by this sign, because we knew that we had been reading Watchtower publications to the exclusion of reading the Bible. Later on we actually counted up all of the material that the organization expected JWs to read. The books, magazines, lessons, etc. added up to over three thousand pages each year—compared with less than two hundred pages of Bible reading assigned—and most of that was in the Old Testament. The majority of Witnesses were so bogged down by the three thousand pages of the organization's literature that they seldom got around to doing the Bible reading.

After seeing the picket sign Penni turned to me and said, "We should be reading the Bible *and* the Watchtower material." I agreed, so we began doing regular personal Bible reading with the aim of becoming better Jehovah's Witnesses.

But as we read the New Testament we became impressed with Jesus as a person: what he said and did, how he treated people. We wanted to be his followers. Especially we were struck with how Jesus responded to the hypocritical religious leaders of the day, the scribes and Pharisees. I remember reading over and over again the accounts relating how the Pharisees objected to Jesus' healing on the Sabbath, his disciples' eating with unwashed hands, and other details of behavior that violated their traditions. How I loved Jesus' response: "You hypocrites, Isaiah aptly prophesied about you, when he said, 'This people honors me with their lips, yet their heart is far removed from me. It is in vain that they keep worshiping me, because they teach commands of men as doctrines'" (Matt. 15:7–9, Watchtower's *New World Translation*).

Commands of men as doctrines! That thought stuck in my mind, and I began to realize that, in fulfilling my role as an elder, I was acting more like a Pharisee than a follower of Jesus. For example, the elders were the enforcers of all sorts of petty rules about dress and grooming, and this reminded me of the Pharisees who condemned Jesus' disciples for eating with unwashed hands.

Grooming was not the real issue, however. For me it was a question of whose disciple I was. Was I a follower of Jesus, or an obedient servant to a human hierarchy? The elders who eventually put me on trial knew that that was the real issue, too. They kept asking, "Do you believe that the Watchtower Society is God's organization? Do you believe that the Society speaks as Jehovah's mouthpiece?"

With the new perspective that I was gaining from Bible reading, it upset me to see the organization elevate itself above
Scripture, as it did when the December 1, 1981, *Watchtower* said:
"Jehovah God has also provided his visible organization. . . .
Unless we are in touch with this channel of communication that
God is using, we will not progress along the road to life, no matter
how much Bible reading we do" (p. 27). It really disturbed me to
see those men elevate themselves above God's Word. Since I was
not allowed to speak out at the meetings, I decided to try writing.
That's when I started publishing the newsletter *Comments from
the Friends.*

The elders wanted to put me on trial for publishing it, but my
wife and I simply stopped going to the Kingdom Hall. By that
time most of our former friends there had become quite hostile
toward us. One young man called on the phone and threatened
to "come over and take care of" me if he got another newsletter.
And another Witness actually left a couple of death threats on
our answering machine.

It was a great relief to be out from under the oppressive yoke
of that organization. But, we now had to face the challenge of
where to go and what to believe. It takes some time to rethink
your entire religious outlook on life. And we had not yet come
into fellowship with Christians outside the JW organization.

All Penni and I knew was that we wanted to follow Jesus and
that the Bible contained all the information we needed. We were
amazed at what we found in prayerfully reading the New Testament over and over again—things that we had never appreciated
before, like the closeness that the early disciples enjoyed with the
risen Lord, the activity of the Holy Spirit in the early church, and
Jesus' words about being born again.

All those years we were Jehovah's Witnesses, the Watchtower
had taken us on a guided tour through the Bible. We gained a lot
of knowledge about the Old Testament, and we could quote a lot
of Scripture, but we never heard the gospel of salvation in Christ.
We never learned to depend on Jesus for our salvation and to look
to him personally as our Lord. Everything centered around the
Watchtower's works program, and people were expected to come
to Jehovah God through the organization.

When I realized from reading Romans 8 and John 3 that I
needed to be born of the Spirit, I was afraid at first. Jehovah's
Witnesses believe that born-again people who claim to have the
Holy Spirit are actually possessed by demons. And so I feared that
if I prayed out loud to turn my life over to Jesus Christ, some
demon might be listening, and the demon might jump in and possess me, pretending to be the Holy Spirit. (Many Jehovah's
Witnesses live in constant fear of the demons. Some of our friends
would even throw out second-hand furniture and clothing, fearing that the demons could enter their homes through those articles.) But then I read Jesus' words in Luke 11:9–13 (NKJ). In a
context where he was teaching about prayer and casting out
unclean spirits, Jesus said: "And I say to you, ask, and it will be
given to you; seek, and you will find; knock, and it will be opened
to you. For everyone who asks receives, and he who seeks finds,
and to him who knocks it will be opened. If a son asks for bread
from any of you who is a father, will he give him a stone? Or if he
asks for a fish, will he give him a serpent instead of a fish? Or if
he asks for an egg, will he offer him a scorpion? If you then, being
evil, know how to give good gifts to your children, how much
more will your heavenly Father give the Holy Spirit to those who
ask Him!"

I knew, after reading those words, that I could safely ask for
Christ's Spirit (Rom. 8:9), without fearing that I would receive a
demon. So, in the early morning privacy of our kitchen, I proceeded to confess my need for salvation and to commit my life to
Christ.

Penni teaches fifth grade now in a Christian school that has
students from about seventeen different churches. She really
enjoys it, because she can tie the Scriptures in to all sorts of subjects. And I publish *Comments from the Friends* as a quarterly
aimed at reaching Jehovah's Witnesses with the gospel and help-
ing Christians who are talking to JWs.

Although the thrust of my outreach ministry is toward
Jehovah's Witnesses, I also take advantage of opportunities to
share the gospel with Mormons and have had numerous conversations with them—on the street when they were canvassing for
potential converts, and in my home when I have accepted their

offer of a free copy of the Book of Mormon, which they personally deliver as a way to start weekly discussions. My research on Mormonism started out as preparation for such visits by the missionaries.

The most important lesson Penni and I have learned since leaving the Jehovah's Witnesses is that Jesus is not just a historical figure that we read about. He is alive and is actively involved with Christians today, just as he was back in the first century. He personally saves us, teaches us, and leads us. This personal relationship with God through his Son Jesus Christ is wonderful! The individual who knows Jesus and follows him will not even think about following anyone else: "And a stranger will they not follow, but will flee from him: for they know not the voice of strangers. . . . My sheep hear my voice, and I know them, and they follow me: And I give unto them eternal life; and they shall never perish, neither shall any man pluck them out of my hand" (John 10:5, 27, 28).

Notes

Introduction

1. For specific references see "Subject Index."
2. Doctrine and Covenants 132:61–62

Chapter 3 *Mormon Scripture*

1. Not to be confused with his other novel *Manuscript Story*.
2. *A Marvelous Work And A Wonder*, 1979 edition, p. 79.
3. This edition also contained a section titled "Lectures on Faith," included in all editions until 1921 but then quietly removed without a common consent vote of the membership. The 1844 edition added seven revelations. In 1876, twenty-six additional reveltions were added, many predated, having to do with priesthood authority. These were not voted on by common consent of the membership until October 1880.

Chapter 4 *Verse-by-Verse Answers for Mormons: Old Testament*

1. In actuality, the LDS Church teaches the existence of a whole pantheon of Gods, but links these three together in relation to the planet Earth: "Heavenly Father, Jesus Christ, and the Holy Ghost are called the *Godhead*. They are unified in purpose" (*Gospel Principles*, LDS Church, 1986 edition, p. 34).
2. *Gospel Principles* (LDS Church, Salt Lake City, 1986), p. 34.
3. Rather than proving God the Father has a body of flesh and bones, this verse is speaking of the LORD (Jehovah), who to Mormons is the premortal Jesus (at this time a personage of Spirit), not God the Heavenly Father.
4. *Articles of Faith* by James E. Talmage (LDS Church, Salt Lake City, 1952 printing), pp. 467 and 472, quoting an official declaration, "The Father and The Son: A Doctrinal Exposition by The First Presidency and The Twelve" (1916).
5. *Articles of Faith*, p. 42.
6. Joseph F. Smith, "The Origin of Man," *Improvement Era*, Nov. 1909, pp. 78, 80, quoted in *Gospel Principles* (LDS Church, Salt Lake City, 1986), p. 9.
7. *Gospel Principles* (LDS Church, Salt Lake City, 1986), p. 6.
8. *Teachings of the Prophet Joseph Smith* compiled by Joseph Fielding Smith (Deseret Book Company, Salt Lake City, 1976 ed.) p. 373.

Notes

140

9. *Articles of Faith*, page 473.

10. "Fall of Adam," LDS *Bible Dictionary* (1979, 1990 printing), p. 670.

11. Copies may be found reproduced in *Mormonism—Shadow or Reality?* by Jerald and Sandra Tanner (Modern Microfilm Co., Salt Lake City, 1972), pages 173–178D; also in *"And this is Life Eternal that they might know Thee, the only true God" and ?Adam?* by Melaine Layton (self-published) pages 39–47. For information on how to obtain these books send a stamped self-addressed long envelope to: Berean Christian Ministries, P. O. Box 1091, Webster, NY 14580.

Chapter 5 Verse-by-Verse Answers for Mormons: New Testament

1. A Mormon may object that these verses are not translated correctly. If such an objection is encountered, a reading of Alma 7:10 will prove helpful, since the Book of Mormon there agrees with the Bible on the role of the Holy Ghost.

2. *A Marvelous Work And A Wonder*, by LeGrand Richards, 1979 edition, pp. 115, 117; also, see Doctrine and Covenants 130:22.

3. Verse numbers vary somewhat from the King James Version due to Smith's insertion of additional material.

4. *A Marvelous Work And A Wonder*, by LeGrand Richards, 1979 edition, p. 60.

5. The Mormon Church in Doctrine and Covenants 13:1 implies that such animal sacrifices will be resumed in the future. This verse has John the Baptist saying to Joseph Smith and his companion, "Upon you my fellow servants, in the name of the Messiah I confer the Priesthood of Aaron . . . and this shall never be taken again from the earth, until the sons of Levi do offer again an offering unto the Lord in righteousness."

6. See the discussions of Genesis 1:26, 27; 2:7; and Luke 1:34, 35, which reveal the "Father" and "God" Mormons worship.

7. The problem stems from the fact that Mormons are taught that God, men, angels, and demons are all of the same nature, or species. To Christians, God, men, angels, and demons have different natures, just as dogs differ from cats. To Mormons, men can become angels and Gods. To Christians, the Father, Son, and Holy Ghost are the only ones having the same divine nature, thereby are *one* God.

8. According to the interlinear reading of *The Zondervan Parallel New Testament in Greek and English* (Grand Rapids: Zondervan Bible Publishers, 1981).

9. For example: 1 Cor. 15:12; 2 Cor. 11:4, 5; Gal. 3:1; Eph. 4:14; Phil. 1:15–17; 2 Thess. 2:1–12; 1 Tim. 4:1–3; 2 Tim. 4:3, 4; Titus 1:11; James 2:18–20; 2 Peter 2:1–22, 3:16; 1 John 2:18, 19; 2 John 8–11; 3 John 9, 10; Jude 3, 4.

10. Preceding the 1832 revelation was the dedication of the temple site and the setting of a stone marker on August 3, 1831 (*Times and Seasons*, vol. 5, no. 5, p. 450).

11. A modern Christian scholar agreed with Smith's thought. See *Encylopedia of Biblical Difficulties* by Gleason F. Archer (Grand Rapids: Zondervan, 1982).

12. Since Mormons have been taught that "the LORD" (YHWH, Yahweh, Jehovah) is the antemortal name of Jesus Christ, and does not designate God the Father, they have a problem when they trace its New Testament references to their origin in Psalm 110. According to Mormon teachings it is Jesus who says, "Sit thou on my right hand." But Jesus himself said, "To sit on my right hand, and on my left, is not mine to give, but it shall be given to them for whom it is prepared of my Father" (Matt. 20:23).

Chapter 6: Verse-by-Verse Answers for Mormons: Book of Mormon

1. To obtain more information on these items and unusual and unique teachings in the Book of Mormon, please send a self-addressed, stamped, long envelope to Berean Christian Ministries, P. O. Box 1091, Webster, NY 14580.

2. Remains of extinct miniature horses (the size of dogs) have been found in North American tar pits, but the presence of these distant relatives of modern horses does not fit the Book of Mormon account.

3. Brigham Young, 1857, *Journal of Discourses*, vol. 4, p. 218.

4. The 1835 edition of Doctrine and Covenants included an approved article on "Marriage," Section CI (101). Verse 4 said: "Inasmuch as this church of Christ has been reproached with the crime of fornication, and polygamy: we declare that we believe, that one man should have one wife; and one woman, but one husband." This was included in all editions until 1876, when it was quietly removed. Smith's 1843 "revelation" advocating polygamy was then inserted as Doctrine and Covenants Section 132, becoming part of canonized Mormon scripture in 1880, just ten years before the practice was officially discontinued. Therefore, during the period from the 1830s to 1876 when Mormons were practicing plural marriage, Doctrine and Covenants included a section condemning it; and during the post polygamy period from 1890 onward, Doctrine and Covenants has included a section advocating the practice.

5. In the 1982 revision of Doctrines and Covenants, the 1890 Manifesto was renamed "Official Declaration 1," and the 1978 statement giving the priesthood to blacks became "Official Declaration 2."

6. See the rendering of Isaiah 53, verse 1, at John 12:38 and Romans 10:16; verse 4 at Matthew 8:17; verses 5, 6 at 1 Peter 2:24, 25; verses 7, 8 at Acts 8:32, 33; verse 9 at 1 Peter 2:22; and verse 12 at Luke 22:37.

Chapter 7: Some Techniques for Sharing the Gospel with Mormons

1. A recent policy change has money for missionaries channeled through Mormon Church headquarters in Salt Lake City.

2. See the discussion under Nehemiah 9:6 for additional details.

Chapter 8: Testimonies of the Authors

1. Mormons who have been through the temple for their "endowments" are required to wear "temple garments" continually from that time forward. The original temple garment consisted of a one-piece white union suit reaching from the neck to the wrists and ankles. Shortened sleeves and legs are now approved. The garments have four symbolic markings: a square on the right breast and a compass on the left, a stitched line over the navel and right knee. Masons have said that these breast markings remind them of the square and the compass pressed against the body in those locations during Masonic rituals.

Recommended Reading

Mormon "Sacred Scripture" or "Standard Works"

The Holy Bible, Authorized King James Version with Explanatory Notes and Cross References to the Standard Works of the Church of Jesus Christ of Latter-day Saints (Salt Lake City: The Church of Jesus Christ of Latter-day Saints, 1990)

Book of Mormon (Salt Lake City: The Church of Jesus Christ of Latter-day Saints, 1990)

Doctrine and Covenants (Salt Lake City: The Church of Jesus Christ of Latter-day Saints, 1990)

Pearl of Great Price (Salt Lake City: The Church of Jesus Christ of Latter-day Saints, 1990)

Other Mormon Publications

A Marvelous Work And A Wonder, LeGrand Richards (Salt Lake City: Deseret Book Company, 1976 and 1979 editions)

Articles of Faith, James E. Talmage (Salt Lake City: The Church of Jesus Christ of Latter-day Saints, 1952 and 1987 editions)

Gospel Principles, anonymous (Salt Lake City: The Church of Jesus Christ of Latter-day Saints, 1986 edition)

Jesus the Christ: A Study of the Messiah and His Mission According to Holy Scriptures both Ancient and Modern, James E. Talmage (Salt Lake City: Deseret Book Company, 1975)

Mormon Doctrine, Bruce R. McConkie (Salt Lake City: Bookcraft, 2nd edition, 1979)

Mormon Experience, The, Leonard J. Arrington and Davis Bitton (New York: Vintage Books, 1980)

Story of the Latter-day Saints, The, James B. Allen and Glen M. Leonard (Salt Lake City: Deseret Book Company, 1976)

Teachings of the Prophet Joseph Smith, compiled by Joseph Fielding Smith (Salt Lake City: Deseret Book Company, 1976)

Critical Works

Adam-God Maze, The, Culley Christensen, M.D. (Scottsdale, Ariz.: Independent Publishers, 1981)

"And this is Life Eternal that they might know Thee, the only True God" ?Adam?, Melaine Layton (Wheeling, Ill.: self-published, no date)

Answering Mormons' Questions, Bill McKeever (Minneapolis: Bethany House Publishers, 1991)

3,913 Changes in the Book of Mormon: A Photo Reprint of the Original 1830 Edition of The Book of Mormon With all the Changes Marked, Jerald and Sandra Tanner (Salt Lake City: Modern Microfilm Co., no date)

Changing World of Mormonism, The, Jerald and Sandra Tanner (Chicago: Moody Press, 1980)

God's Word, Final, Infallible and Forever, Floyd McElveen (Grand Rapids: Gospel Truths Ministries, 1985)

Kingdom of the Cults, The, Walter R. Martin (Minneapolis: Bethany House Publishers, 1977 edition)

Mormon Claims Answered, Marvin W. Cowan (Salt Lake City: self-published, 1984 and 1989 editions)

Mormon Polygamy—A History, Richard S. Van Wagoner (Salt Lake City: Signature Books, 1986)

Mormonism, Mama, and Me, Thelma "Granny" Geer (Chicago: Moody Press, 1986 edition)

Mormonism—Shadow or Reality?, Jerald and Sandra Tanner (Salt Lake City: Modern Microfilm Company, 1972 enlarged edition)

No Man Knows My History, Fawn M. Brodie (New York: Alfred A. Knopf, 2d ed. 1971)

On the Frontlines Witnessing to Mormons, Wally Tope (La Cañada Flintridge, Calif.: Frontline Ministries, 1981 edition)

Use of the Bible in the Book of Mormon, The, H. Michael Marquardt (St. Louis: Personal Freedom Outreach, 1979)

Where Does It Say That?, Bob Witte (West Bridgewater, Mass.: Ex-Mormons for Jesus, no date [post-1980])

Why We Left Mormonism, Latayne C. Scott (Grand Rapids: Baker Book House, 1990)

Witnessing to the Mormons, Jerry and Marian Bodine (San Juan Capistrano, Calif.: Christian Research Institute, 1978)

Booklets

A Book of Mormon Study (A Christian's View), John R. Farkas (Webster, N.Y.: Berean Christian Ministries, 1989)

Book of Mormon Authorship: A Closer Look, Vernal Holley (Ogden, Utah: Zenos Publications, 1983; also, Roy, Utah: 2nd edition, self-published, 1989)

Does the Mormon Church Attack Orthodox Christianity?, John R. Farkas (St. Louis: Personal Freedom Outreach, 1988)

How to Witness to Mormons, John R. Farkas (Webster, N.Y.: Berean Christian Ministries, no date)

Joseph Smith's Bainbridge, N.Y., Court Trials, Wesley P. Walters (Salt Lake City: Modern Microfilm Company, 1977)

What the Mormons Really Think of Christ and the Father, John R. Farkas (St. Louis: Personal Freedom Outreach, 1988)

Articles

"The Church of Jesus Christ of Latter-day Saints: An Historical Overview," Rick Branch & James Walker, Watchman Expositor, vol. 7, no. 1 (Columbus, Ga.: Watchman Fellowship, 1989)

Subject Index

Aaronic Priesthood. *See* Priesthood
Adam-God doctrine, 22, 41–42, 60–61,
    63, 123, 126
America(s)
    Christ visited, 29, 68, 74
    early inhabitants, 29, 43, 45, 55, 68,
        74, 117, 119
anachronism(s). *See* Book of Mormon
Ancient of days, 22, 24, 41, 59, 60, 61, 62,
    63
angel(s), 30, 40, 44, 97
animals, 37–38, 41, 88, 110, 111, 129
apostle(s), 22, 84–85
archaeology, 107, 110–11
"Articles of Faith, The," 27, 32, 34, 35,
    49, 70, 139, 143. *See Pearl of Great*
    Price
atonement, 24, 87
authority. *See* priesthood
apostasy, 82, 89, 94, 95

Babel, tower of, 43, 119
Bainbridge, New York, 30
baptism, for the dead, 22, 25, 32, 85–86
beliefs, Mormon, 32, 33, 35, 37, 38, 39,
    51, 52, 53, 62, 69, 82, 125
Benson, Ezra Taft, 20
Bible, 13, 22, 27–29, 58
    belief in, 12, 22, 27, 28, 45, 66, 106,
        131
    copied in Book of Mormon, 55, 74,
        105, 111, 112, 115, 116, 118
    errors in, 22, 28, 29
    Joseph Smith Translation, 22, 23, 28,
        29, 34, 101, 103, 115

King James Version, 28, 29, 62, 100,
    105, 112, 115
    reliable, 28, 106–107
blacks, 19, 23, 32, 33, 94, 113
Book of Abraham. 18, 19, 32, 33, 39, 40,
    81, 130. *See Pearl of Great Price*
"Book of Breathings," 19, 33
Book of Commandments, 16, 31, 130
Book of Mormon, 12, 16, 22, 27, 28,
    29–31, 49, 55, 56, 58, 74, 89, 100,
    108, 124, 130
    anachronism(s), 28, 31, 110–12,
        115–116, 117, 118
    archaeology, 107, 110–11
    author, 30, 31, 43, 106, 111, 112, 118
    changes, 130
    familiar spirit, 55, 56
    gold plates, 15, 30, 34, 56, 115
    prayer about, 100, 120
Book of Moses, 32. *See Pearl of Great Price*
Brigham Young University, 12, 18, 20
Buchanan, James, 18

Carthage, Illinois, 17, 63
Christ
    birth of, 69–70
    Mormon view, 40, 45, 51, 69, 71
    pre-existence, 52, 53
    resurrection of, 29, 53, 70–71, 86
church(es)
    Christian, 49, 67, 84, 85, 102, 108,
        109
    Church of Jesus Christ of Latter-day
        Saints, 16, 19, 21, 41

LDS, 11, 12, 16, 24, 28, 33, 38, 39, 49,
    53, 54, 64, 69, 108, 124, 125, 129
Mormon Church, 12, 34
Reorganized Church of Jesus Christ of
    Latter Day Saints, 18, 28, 29, 34
clothing. *See* temple garment
compass
    mariner's, 110
    on temple garment, 141
Congress, U.S., 11, 12, 19, 113
Cowdery, Oliver, 16, 31, 34, 77
creation, 41
Cumorah. *See* Hill Cumorah

Deseret Book Company, 27, 29
doctrine, 12, 22–25, 27, 29, 32, 35, 37, 41,
    51, 61, 69, 70, 73, 76, 83, 105
    authority, 88, 95, 96, 98
    changes, 21, 27, 28, 29, 61, 69, 103
    sources. *See Pearl of Great Price.*
Doctrine and Covenants, 16, 31–32, 63, 71,
    72, 81

Edmunds Act, 19, 113
Egypt, Egyptian
    hieroglypics, 33, 39
    papyrus, 19, 33, 39
    reformed Egyptian, 30, 34, 115, 116
eternal progression, 23
Eve, 22, 32, 41, 60
Expositor. See Nauvoo Expositor
Fillmore, Millard, 18
First Vision, 15, 34, 72, 108

gentile(s), 12, 74, 75, 113, 117
glass looker. *See* Smith, Joseph
God, gods
    Adam-God. *See* Adam-God doctrine
    Ancient of days. *See* Ancient of days
    body, 23, 37–38, 39, 44, 46–48, 49–50,
        51, 69, 71, 90, 96–97, 105
    Elohim, 23, 24, 46, 50, 51, 60
    Father, has a, 105
    Father, the, 23, 42, 59, 66, 67
    Holy Ghost, 65–66, 67
    Holy Spirit, 40, 46, 67
    Jehovah, 24, 45–46, 50–51, 59, 60, 91
    men may become, 68, 82, 85, 90, 105,
        118

Michael, the Archangel, 22, 24, 41,
    59, 60, 62
    name of, 23, 24, 46, 49, 50, 51
    of this planet, 41
    one, 37, 39, 42, 51, 52, 67, 80, 83–84
    once a man, 47, 68, 118
    plurality of, 12, 33, 37, 39, 40, 42, 46,
        54, 67, 75, 83–84, 90, 125
    procreation, 7, 33, 39, 40, 46, 53–54,
        59, 67, 79–80, 105
    resurrected, 71, 86
    three, 37, 39, 53
    Trinity, 39, 40, 46, 59, 67, 79–80
    wife, wives of, 41, 105
godhead, 47
gold plates. *See* Book of Mormon
gospel, another, 81, 89, 90, 91, 109
governor of Utah. *See* Smith, Joseph;
    Young, Brigham
grace, 81

heaven
    levels, 23, 87, 88, 105
hell, 23
Hill Cumorah, 15, 30, 132
horse(s). *See* animals
husband(s). *See* Mary

Indians, 11, 18
Inspired Version. *See* Bible, Joseph Smith
    Translation

jail, 17, 114
Jehovah, 24, 45–46, 50–51, 59, 60
Jesus Christ. *See* Christ, Jesus
John the Baptist, 16, 77

King James Version. *See* Bible
Kolob, 33

Laman, Lamanites, 74
Lee, John D., 18

Manchester, New York, 15
manifesto, 12, 19, 113, 114
marriage
    celestial, 24, 25, 32, 85, 90, 114
    God married, 53, 69
    polygamy, 11, 12, 16, 17, 18, 19, 21,
        24, 32, 64, 69, 94, 112–14

Mary, 53, 66, 68, 69, 105
    more than one husband, 69
massacre
    Haun's Mill Massacre, 16
    Mountain Meadows Massacre, 11, 18
Melchizedek Priesthood. *See* priesthood
militia, 11, 18
Mormon Church
    founded, 16, 17, 34
    history, 16, 17
    membership, 12, 18, 19, 20
    names of, 16, 18, 21
Mormon Tabernacle Choir, 11
Moroni, 15, 30, 34, 102
Morrill Act, 18
Mountain Meadows Massacre, 11, 18

name(s)
    of God, 23, 24, 46, 49, 50, 51
    of Mormon Church, 16, 18, 21
Nauvoo, Illinois, 11, 17, 113
Nauvoo Expositor, 17
Nephi, Nephites, 30, 55, 95, 111, 117. *See also* "Scripture Index"

Palmyra, New York, 16, 30, 131
papyrus. *See* Egypt
Pearl of Great Price, 18, 27, 28, 28, 32–35, 39, 92, 124. *See also Book of Abraham; Book of Moses; Doctrine and Covenants*
peep-stone. *See* Smith, Joseph, Jr.
persecution, 108, 112
polygamy. *See* marriage
pre-existence
    of Christ, 52, 53, 76
    of humans, 25, 32, 57, 61, 76, 80–81
priesthood
    Aaronic, 16, 34, 47, 77–78
    authority, 76–77
    blacks, 19, 23, 33, 113
    Jesus Christ, 43
    Melchizedek, 16, 43, 54, 72, 77, 78–79, 99
    Mormon, 76–77, 78, 79
    restoration, 77, 78, 79, 82, 99, 102
prophecy(ies), 44, 45, 48, 49, 55, 63, 79
    false prophecies, 91–95

prophet(s), 21, 47, 48, 63, 64, 91, 94, 96, 114

Reorganized Church of Jesus Christ of Latter Day Saints. *See* churches
restoration
    authority, 13, 84, 95, 96, 97–98, 99, 102
    priesthood, 76–77, 78, 79, 89, 97–98, 102
resurrection of the dead, 23, 24, 86
Richards, LeGrand, 28, 31, 49, 55, 70, 76, 77
RLDS. *See* Reorganized Church of Jesus Christ of Latter Day Saints

Salt Lake City, Utah, 17, 113
Satan, 32, 100
Scripture
    changes to, 29, 71
    See also Book of Mormon; Bible, the Holy; *Doctrine and Covenants; Pearl of Great Price*
Shiz, 119
Smith, Joseph, Jr., 34, 39, 89, 130
    author, 16, 30, 36
    glass looker, 15, 30, 31, 56
    jailed, 17
    killed, 11, 17, 63
    lieutenant-general, 17
    mayor, 17
    peep-stone, 15, 30
    revelation(s), 17, 30, 31, 32, 47, 71–72, 73, 80, 87, 90, 113, 114
    translation(s), 23, 28, 29, 30, 33, 34, 39, 56, 72, 101–2, 103, 115, 116
    visions(s), 15, 34, 72, 108
Smithsonian Institution, 110
Spalding, Solomon, 31
Spirit. *See* God
spirit(s)
    pre-existence as, 32, 61, 76, 80–81
standard works. *See* Scripture
star. *See* Kolob
statistics, 12, 17, 18, 19, 20
sticks of Judah, 58–59

temple, 16
    ceremonies, 12, 22, 24, 25, 85

garments, 12, 22, 130
recommend, 12, 22, 24
Thummim. See Urim and Thummim
translation(s). See Bible; Smith, Joseph, Jr.
Trinity. See God

Urim and Thummim, 30
Utah
governor, 18
migration to, 11
statehood, 12, 17, 19, 24, 64, 94, 113
territory, 11, 113

Utah War, 18

war. See Utah War
witnesses, two, 88–89
witnessing, 124–25
Woodruff, Wilford. See manifesto

Young, Brigham
Adam-God teaching, 41–42, 60–62
Brigham Young University, 12, 18
governor of Utah, 11, 18
migration to Utah, 11, 17

Scripture Index

Genesis

1:1, 3—50
1:16—47
1:24, 25—37
1:26—38
1:26, 27—37, 39,
  40, 42, 44, 48,
  50, 51, 67, 80
1:27—47
2:7—40, 52, 63
2:22—41
2:24—114
3:8-13—125
6:9—67
11:7—42, 119
11:8, 9—43
11:9—119
14—78-79
14:18—43, 79
27:20—46
32:1—44
32:24—44
32:30—38, 44, 47,
  48, 50, 72, 80
37:5—44, 68
37:10—44, 68
42:6—45
42:9—45

Exodus

Book of, 78
3:4—47
3:6, 7—46
4:14—77

4:16—54, 77
6:3—45, 51, 52, 53
24:10, 11—44, 46,
  48, 50, 72
28:1—77
33:9—47
33:11—38, 44, 47,
  47, 50, 72
33:20—47, 48
33:22—44, 72
33:22, 23—48

Leviticus

Book of, 78

Numbers

Book of, 78
12:6-8—48

Deuteronomy

Book of, 78
1:32, 33—45
4:2—48, 49, 49,
  72, 103
4:28—44, 48, 49,
  50
6:4—46, 50, 52,
  53
8:9-12—56
8:20-22—93
18:15—111
18:18, 19—111
18:20-22—91

1 Kings

8:27—50

1 Chronicles

10:13—56

2 Chronicles

33:6—56

Nehemiah

9:6—51, 53, 83

Job

1:1—68
38:4—57
40:3-5—57

Psalms

2:7—52-53, 70
8:5—40
41:13—50
82—53-54, 75
82:1—53, 54
82:2—54
82:3—54
82:5—54
82:6—53, 75
82:7—54
82:8—54
93:2—52
94:9—50
103:17—52

106:48—50
110:1—97
110:4—44, 54, 79
147:4, 5—52

Proverbs

14:12—100

Isaiah

29:1—55
29:1-4—55
29:4—55
29:11—55
40:8—107
43:3—45
43:10—52, 83
43:11—45
44—53
44:6—52, 53, 83,
  127
44:8—52, 53, 127
44:21—52
44:24—52
45:5, 6—52
46:9—52
46:10—57
48:17—45
53—115
53:1—115
53:2—115
53:3—115
64:6—67
64:8—81

151

Jeremiah

1:5—57, 76, 81
30:2—49

Ezekiel

3:18, 19—124
37:16, 17—58
37:18—58
37:21, 22—58
37:22—59

Daniel

7:9—42, 52, 59,
  62, 70
7:9–14—62
7:13—42, 59, 62
7:14—62
7:22—42, 59, 62

Hosea

11:9—50
12:4—44

Amos

3:7—63–64, 85

Zechariah

4:6—124
12:1—57

Malachi

2:10—81
3:16—62

Matthew

1:18—65, 70
1:18–20—53
1:20—65, 70
3:16, 17—40, 66,
  67, 80
5:48—67, 68, 83
6—116
6:14—116
6:24—116
7:15—12
10:5, 6—68

12:18—75
12:21—75
15:7–9—134
15:9—109
15:22–28—74
15:24—45, 68, 74,
  75
16:18—82
19:4–9—114
23:39—34
23:39–41—34
24—34
24:1–56—34
24:34—92
28:19, 20—124

Mark

12:28, 29—50
13:30—92

Luke

1:34, 35—53, 66,
  68–69
2:11—45
2:36—74
4:9–12—100
6:13—85
11:9–13—136
16:16—96
18:27—57
22:25, 26—98
22:48—125
24:31—71
24:36—71
24:39—70, 71
24:44, 45—107

John

1:12—98
1:18—44, 47, 48,
  71, 73, 80, 102
1:19—72
3:13—76
3:16—131
4:24—38
6:41, 42—73
6:45–47—73
6:46—72–73

6:51—73
6:57—73
6:62—73
10:5—137
10:16—45, 68, 73,
  74, 117
10:26, 27—118
10:27, 28—137
10:33—75
10:34—54, 75
16:12—127
17—40
17:5—58, 76, 81,
  83
18:4—125
18:37—117
20:19—71
20:26—71
35:36—75

Acts

1:2—107
1:25, 26—85
2:36—74
3:20, 21—76, 79,
  102
3:21—44, 77
3:22, 23—111
7—80
7:55, 56—79, 80
9:15—75
10:45—117
11:1, 2—117
13:33, 34—53
17:11—101
17:28, 29—58,
  76, 80, 83
20:30—81, 82,
  102
28:28—75

Romans

3:10—67
3:23—67
3:24—45
4:17—57
8:8, 9—83
8:9—101, 136

8:15—82, 83
8:16, 17—81, 82
8:17—83
10:19—74
10:29—74
11:1—74

1 Corinthians

1:10—86
3:1—86
3:6—123
3:9—123
5:1—86
5:9—85
8:4—54, 83, 84
8:5—54, 83–84
8:6—84
8:7—84
10:1–4—45
10:13—67
11:19—86
11:21—86
12–14—86
12:28—84—96
12:28–31—79
15—86
15:29—85—86
15:35—88
15:35–53—71
15:39—88
15:40–42—87
15:43—88
15:45—41
15:46—57
15:47—41

2 Corinthians

3:18—38
5:7—99
10:4, 5—127
13:1—88, 101

Galatians

1:6—89, 109
1:6–8—81
1:7—89, 109
1:8—30, 82, 102
3:1, 2—89

4:5, 6—83
4:6—71
5:1—116

Ephesians
3:17—71
4:11—85, 91

Philippians
1:17—109
2:6, 7—38

Colossians
1:27—71
2:9—71
4:6—109

1 Thessalonians
5:21—101, 109

2 Thessalonians
2:3—82, 102

1 Timothy
1:3, 4—86
2:5—53
3:12—85, 114
3:2—114
4:1, 2—82, 102

2 Timothy
3:15-17—107
4:2-4—124

Titus
3:9—86

Hebrews
1:1, 2—85, 96
1:3—38, 80, 96
1:5—53
1:13—97
4:4-7—107
4:7—118
5—54, 79, 99
5:1—97
5:4—97
5:5—53
5:6—44, 98, 102
5:12-14—127
5:14—109, 124, 132
6—54, 99
6:20—79
7—54, 99
7:1—98, 102
7:23—43
7:24—43, 54

7:24, 25—79
7:25—43
8—54, 99
8:1—99
8:11—98
8:13—78
9:1—78
9:9-28, 78
10:1-8—78
10:9, 10—78
11:1—99
11:27—99
13:8—118

James
1:5—99-100
1:17—118

1 Peter
1:23-25—107
1:25—95
2:5—98
2:9—98
3:14—124

2 Peter
2:1—109
3:15, 16—107

1 John
1:8-10—67
2:27—98
3:2—71
4:1—101
4:12—72, 73, 101

Jude
3—109, 124

Revelation
Book of, 103
1:4—62
1:5, 6—98
1:14-16—80
2:14, 15—89
2:20-24—89
3:21—62
5:11—62
7:10—62
7:15—62
11:18—62
14:5—62
19:20—62
20:10—62
20:12—62
22:1—62
22:18—48, 49, 102-103

Mormon Scripture Index

Book of Mormon

1 Nephi

3:24–27—91
3:26–29—22, 28
4:10—107–108
6:10, 16—109–10
6:16—109–10
10:18—118
13:24–27—106
16:10—111
16:16—111
18:12—110
18:21—110
18:25—110, 129
19:23—111
22:20—111, 116, 118

2 Nephi

5:12—110
5:15—110
9:38—87
26:11—87
26:15–17—55
31:8—111–12
31:10—111–12

Jacob

2:26, 27—112, 113

Mosiah

6:25–27—87
9:9—110
14—115, 116
14:1—115
14:2—115
14:3—115
16:5—87

16:11—87

Alma

1:29—110
4:6—110
5:28—87
34:31–35—87
37:38—110
58:40—115, 118

3 Nephi

Book of, 116–18
13—116
13:14—115, 116
13:24—115, 116
15—74, 117
15:17—45, 68, 74, 116–17
15:21, 22—45, 68, 74, 116–17
15:23—117
16—74, 117
28:1–8—95

Mormon

9:8, 9—118

Ether

1–15—119
1:33–37–43, 119
7:9—110
9:19—110
15:29–31—119

Moroni

10:4—100, 120

Doctrine and Covenants

27:11—59, 62
67:11—72
84:3, 4—92
84:21, 22—72
116:1—62
132:20—82
138:38—60

Pearl of Great Price

Moses

3:5—32
4:1—32
5:11—33
6:51—32
6:64, 65—33

Abraham

1:21–26—33
3:3—33
3:9—33
4:1—33
4:26, 27—39

Joseph Smith—Matthew

1:34—92

Joseph Smith—History

1:19—108

"Articles of Faith"

1:8—27, 32, 34, 35